Black White Red

David Bailes
Black White Red
A poetic history of Central Australia

I dedicate this book to my late cousin and elder brother Billy 'Harbour' Bailes. Billy loved the land, his culture and his people. Billy was the link between the Black and White sides of our family and was much loved and highly respected by all.

Aboriginal and Torres Strait Islander readers are warned that this book contains images and references to deceased persons.

Black White Red: A poetic history of Central Australia
ISBN 978 1 76109 160 5
Copyright © text David Bailes 2021
Cover photo: Billy Bailes on his horse Silver at Macumba Station, far north of South Australia, c. 1980 (photo used with the kind permission of his surviving family members)
Cover design: Anna Maria Bailes

First published 2021 by
GINNINDERRA PRESS
PO Box 3461 Port Adelaide 5015
www.ginninderrapress.com.au

Contents

Acknowledgements	7

1 Manta – Land Wangka – Language Tjukur – Dreaming

Invitation to Mparntwe – Alice Springs	15
Simpson Desert Morning	17
Ngintaka and Milpali: a Dreaming Story	19
The Song Lines of Ngintaka	21
Western Desert Dreaming	24
Tjintu Irititja – A Day Long Ago	28
Kapi Wiya – Without Water	31
Tracks and Trails of the Centre	32

2 European Settlement: the Coming of the Piranpa, White People

The Saga of Squatter John	37
The Ballad of Old Bill	48
Love Story from the Lands of Ngintaka	53
Simpson Desert Crossing, 1936	56
Cooper the Cattleman (1895–1963)	59
Bush Christmas, circa 1930	73
Accident at Eringa, 1946	76
Flight to the Spring of Ngintaka	78
The Long Journey of Billy the Stockman	80

3 Assimilation and the Impact of the 'Stolen Generations'

Patrol 235 Charlotte Waters	97
Boy From the Centre in the North	100
2008, Reunion and Reconciliation	102
June and the 'Stolen Generations'	105
Vale Cousin June	115

4 Reunion and Reflection

The Finke Mob	119
Black Man/White Man – Red Blood	123
Conversations with My Late Brother Billy	126
The Stockman's Funeral at Oodnadatta	128
Reflections of a Bush Poet	130
Appendix	131
Glossary	134
Bibliography and Further Reading	140

Acknowledgements

I would like to acknowledge that this book was written on Kaurna land and I respect the Kaurna people, their land, their elders and their cultural beliefs.

There are many people I would like to thank for their help and encouragement with writing my book.

I would like to thank Adele Pring for suggesting to me at a Reconciliation conference that I should write a book about the history of our family.

I spent many hours talking and visiting our Aboriginal family. Billy Bailes, late of Oodnadatta, gave me valuable insights into the history of our family especially from an Aboriginal perspective. Billy taught me many words from Anangu language and introduced me to our extended family. Billy's children and in-laws have been very supportive. Billy's daughter Donna has often been a willing go-between and assisted me with email and phone contacts. Billy's late sister June Bailes and older brother Len Bell (Bailes) helped me understand the complex problems associated with being part of the 'Stolen Generations'. My kangkuru – elder sister/cousin – the late Mona Tur (Kennedy) made many suggestions and corrections to my bilingual poems. Her expertise with Anangu language and particularly with Yankunytjatjara was greatly appreciated.

Jude Aquilina gave me positive feedback as I began the project – thank you, Jude. In the early stages of writing, I appreciated the encouragement of my brother-in-law Yevgeny Seleznev, Marni Morrow and Geoff Connell. My fellow poet Martin Christmas has been very supportive, as has my friend David Weston. Graham Rowlands, an established poet, was a fantastic mentor and edited my manuscript – thanks for all your time, Graham. I would like to thank my friend Roberto Lombardi for his time and expertise with my final proofreading. Daphne Palmer gave her time with editing suggestions – thanks, Daphne.

Many people and old-timers from the stations listened to my questions and helped my understanding of life in the Outback. I would like to especially thank Bruce Delany for giving me information about his time as a stockman working for Cooper Bailes on Eringa station after World War Two.

My parents John Bailes and Marjorie Major assisted my early memories of our family's time in the Northern Territory. My sister Cecilia and her husband Jim Ferry kindly took me to the Centre to meet up with family and visit sites of significance – great driving, Jim, and memorable cooking, Cecilia!

Last and not least, my immediate family were always supportive. Our son Serge was the expert with computer work, our daughter Anna helped with graphic design for the cover and maps. My wife Tanya was very understanding with the time I needed to work on my book.

I would also like to thank Stephen Matthews OAM for his time and patience in publishing my book.

While I have endeavoured to check the accuracy of all poems and their stories, some readers may question some details. I have recorded all information to the best of my ability.

Australia

Areas with a knowledge of Western Desert languages

1. Woomera
2. Coober Pedy
3. Oodnadatta
4. Dalhousie Springs
5. Finke
6. Eringa Station
7. Ernabella/Pukatja
8. Uluru
9. Alice Springs
10. Yuendumu
11. Halls Creek
12. Kalgoorlie

Map of Central Australia with references to places mentioned in the poems

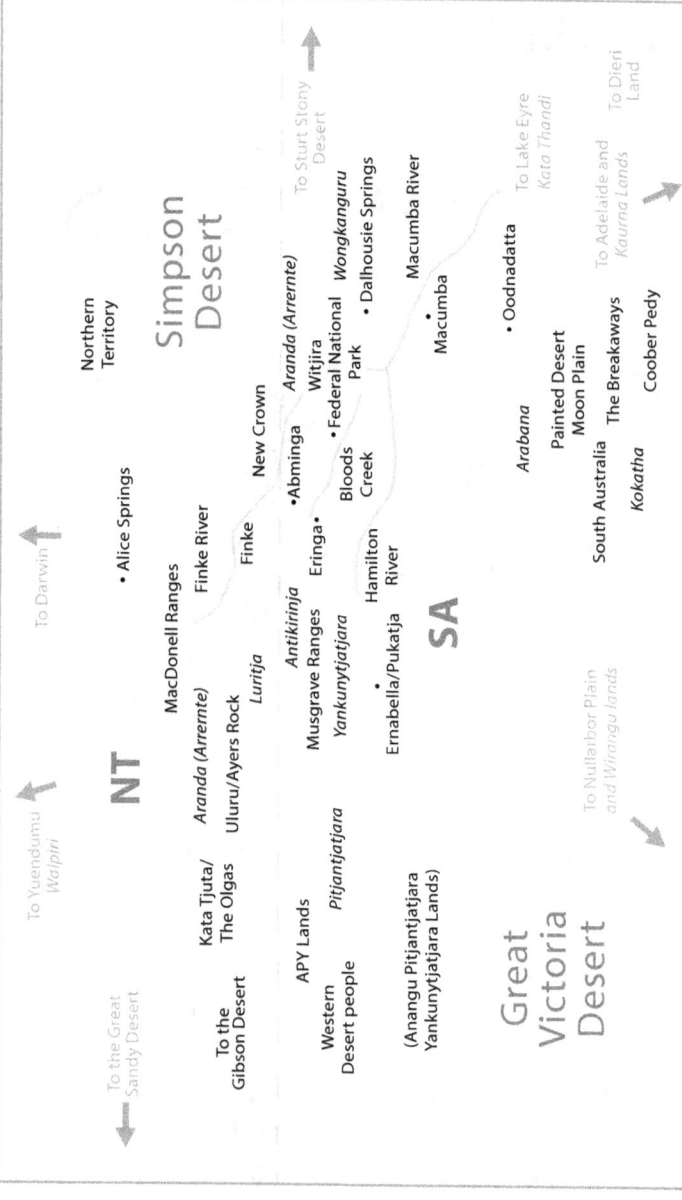

Bailes family tree

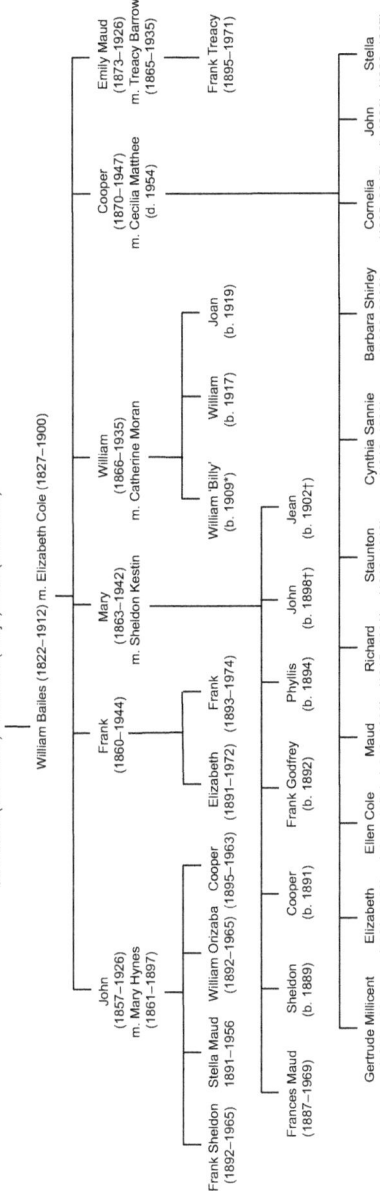

* born to Frances Maud Kestin
† child of John Longwill

Brief Bailes and Cleanskin family tree

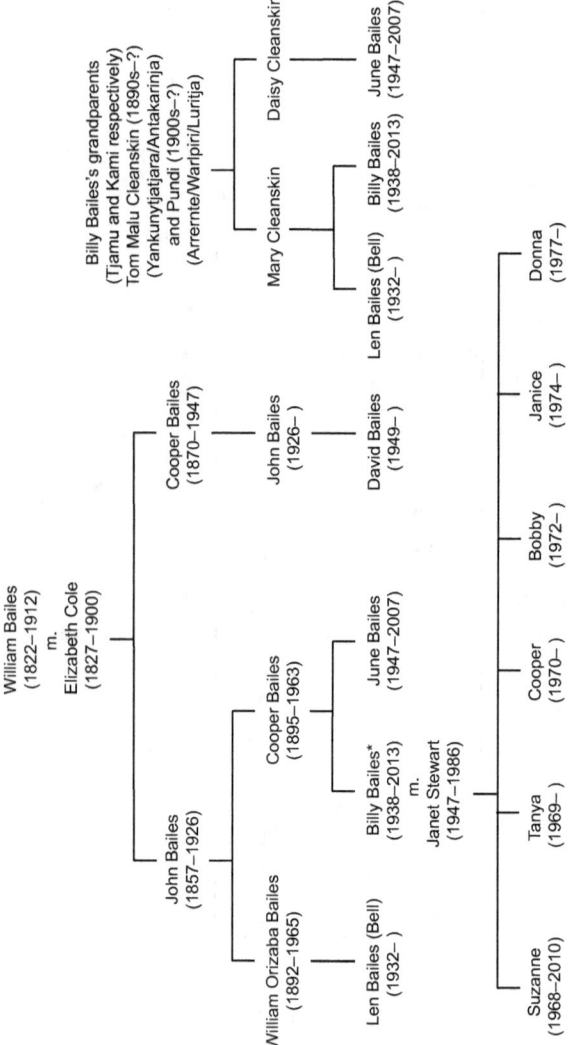

* Before marrying Janet Stewart, Billy had two daughters by Nancy Wing – Alison (d. 2009) and Julie Wing. He also looked after as sons Mark Barry (?) and Phillip Coombes, who were in the care of Nancy. Nancy and her family lived at Finke.

1

Manta – Land
Wangka – Language
Tjukur – Dreaming

Invitation to Mparntwe – Alice Springs

Come with me to another world
beyond closed walls and beyond closed minds.

Leave behind illusory pursuits
and come to a place of inner peace.

Faster than the speed of light
your mind can take you where the spirit is free.

We journey past gleaming ironstone plains
and over oceans of red sand dunes.

Folded mountains sleep like giant goannas
as we come to the lands of the Altyerrenge.

Here in the Dreaming the Ancestor Beings
created the past world with us in the present.

We have arrived and now our feet crunch
through the salty crust on the soft desert sand.

Past clumps of bluebush and yellow salt pans
we appear like pilgrims at a sacred hill.

Winding upwards along a narrow path
we are drawn to a place of meditation.

Here we rest in a shallow cave
where we are at one with the land and all life forms.

Placing our hands on the cave's orange walls
we can feel the strength of the Yeperenye Dreaming.

We are surrounded by stories of an earlier age
when giant stink beetles battled the Caterpillar People.

The defeated Yeperenye formed the ranges and red gums
along Lhere Mparntwe – the place of the river.

In the distance Alhekulyele lifts its purple head
for Mount Gillen was created by fierce fighting dingoes.

Beneath us pink and grey galahs
Slowly move along a timeless valley.

The golden rays of the afternoon sun
drench the ancient Arrernte landscape.

We take a deep breath and slowly exhale
as we take in the Land, the Law and the Dreaming.

This is a journey back and forth in time
that tells who we are and where we are from.

Simpson Desert Morning

The Simpson's long rippled dunes
rise up like giant red waves
set in a sandy sea
that stretches to a blue horizon.

Here the wind has sculpted
the ever-changing curves and contours
of the desert's soft scarlet body
long hidden from curious eyes.

Clumps of yellow spinifex
cling to the base of the sandhills
where tangled cane grass bushes
scatter along the dunes.

Camels and kangaroos shelter
between bluebush and under acacia
where the sand dunes meet the salt flats
only moving once the earth has cooled.

The sun's early rays
warn of the coming heat
but hidden in deep tunnels
the desert wildlife is safe.

Patterned sand goannas
stalk pre-dawn wanderers
for here insects and animals
provide both food and water.

The secretive Eyrean grass wren
hides among the desert grasses
along with strange mice-like marsupials
and cream and orange dragon lizards.

The water-holding frog
with cracked claypan eyes
sleeps in dark suspended animation
awaiting the rains.

All those who enter
this magical domain
sense the calming peace
of the stillness of the quiet desert.

Ngintaka and Milpali: a Dreaming Story

A giant orange and pale yellow lizard
emerges from a remote deserted cave
for this is the beginning in the time of the Dreaming
and this is Ngintaka, the powerful Perentie Man.

Milpali the mischievous sand goanna
is a pastel-coloured young friend of old Ngintaka
and on many a day they are together
in the ever-changing world of the vast inland.

Milpali has learned there will be a corroboree
with rhythmic singing to the beating of sticks
and there many young women will watch and dance
with their bodies lined in ritualistic ochre.

Excitedly Milpali and Ngintaka
make plans of how to impress the girls
and Milpali comes up with a clever idea
of how to paint their transformed bodies.

First Ngintaka would paint Milpali
with an intricate pattern with beautiful lines
and after Milpali would return the favour
so that together they would make a striking pair.

With his usual attention to fine detail
Ngintaka carefully drew on his handsome friend
and he patiently waited for the eager Milpali
to make him look like a man of style.

After painstakingly working on Ngintaka's head
Milpali grew tired of filling in patterns
and quickly daubed great yellow blotches
all along his friend's half finished back.

Milpali reminded Ngintaka they needed to hurry
or all the girls would be taken by other suitors
and as Milpali slipped away from their waterhole
Ngintaka paused to admire his reflection.

Initially old Ngintaka was quietly pleased
but when he turned and looked over his shoulder
he saw on his back the bright yellow circles
that Milpali had painted with impatient haste.

With a great roar Ngintaka reared up
and chased after the scheming, frustrating Milpali
but Milpali heard his angry friend coming
and tunnelled deep in the earth to get far away.

Ngintaka pursued Milpali until he tired
and everywhere he dug down and re-emerged
he created waterholes and made a landscape
that remains to this day for his caring people.

The Song Lines of Ngintaka

Newly formed pink and purple ranges
shimmer beneath an eternal sun
and here the Tjukuritja, the Ancestor Beings,
create all that is and will ever be.

Moving stealthily between the grey-green acacia
comes Wati Ngintaka, the Perentie Lizard Man;
his giant black talons reflect the yellow grasses
and his long forked tongue tests the air.

Old Ngintaka follows a dry watercourse
hiding behind the apara, the river red gums,
until he reaches a place where a billabong
is edged by green reeds and patches of tea tree.

Pink-eared ducks swim on a surface
that mirrors the endless blue liquid sky
and small flocks of nyii-nyii, zebra finches,
cheep as they flit from branch and tree.

Bare feet crunch on the hot desert sand
and happy voices rise and fall
as the fair and dark-haired kungka, women,
laugh as they approach the still waterhole.

Ngintaka blends into the manta land
with fine charcoal lines drawn like intricate shadows
separating the patches of white clay on his sides
from the daubs of untanu, the bright yellow ochre.

The kungka wade into the cooling kapi
and squeal with delight at the water's touch
their bodies glisten with a silver sheen
like a burnished finish on kurku, the dark mulga.

Like two black and gold suns Ngintaka's eyes
sharpen their focus on their innocent prey
and his heartbeat quickens as his forked tongue tastes
the scents of young women unaware of their fate.

Massive black claws seize the fair-haired kungka
as their screams carry to their ngura camp
and Ngintaka places them in his python-like tail
leaving before the wati, men, can gather their spears.

Fleeing to the west across the Witjira
Ngintaka crosses Arrernte and Luritja land
and with one eye he watches over his women
while the other scans for any sign of pursuit.

Revenge is the domain of the Kurdaitcha
and so the masked wood swallow people
paint on their assassins deathly white markings
and fasten on shoes made with blood, down and hair.

Along Bloods Creek are the tjina, tracks of Ngintaka,
for this is his manta land, his Tjukur Dreaming,
but the Kurdaitcha, the silent executioners,
are nearing his shelter in the hills of Eringa.

Ngintaka's kungka need fresh kapi, water,
so Ngintaka uses his magical power
to create a tjukula, a rock waterhole,
known as alkarle, the place of clean water.

The hungry kungka cannot forage for food
so Ngintaka disgorges tjanmata, bulbs,
which multiply quickly providing bush onions
that can now be prepared and cooked over coal.

Ngintaka's tongue warns him the Kurdaitcha are closing
in a land where tjintu, the sun, never sets
but Ngintaka is cunning and creates munga, the darkness,
to allow him to escape with his fair-haired wives.

For millennia the inma – songs – of Ngintaka
tell of his life, travels and creations
and on Tieyon Station the fair-haired kungka
are part of a range of yellow stone hills.

Ngaratjara, the highest peak of the Musgrave Ranges,
is old Ngintaka surveying his lands;
nearby are the fair-haired children and kungka
and the wati, men, who sing of his life.

Western Desert Dreaming

Katanya, the morning star, drips silver on the pale yellow horizon
Kungkarangkalpa, the Seven Sisters flee with the receding
    darkness.
Katjarungkani, the dawn, is breaking across the Western Desert.
Pira kantily, the crescent moon, fades into the blueness of the
    day.

Ngura Tjukuritja, Ngura Waparitja;
the Dreaming places are spread across the manta
Kuwaripatjura – this is the beginning, the time of the
    Ancestor Beings when
ngura iriti, a long time ago, life and land were formed.

Kalaya the emu, collected kaarku, the red brown ochre.
Uluru, the majestic red rock, rises over pila, the sandy plain.
Pali, the boulders, mark Lungkata the lizard's broken body
and holes in apu, the rockface, reveal where the Liru snakes
    threw spears.

Tjanpi, the sharp spinifex, clings to the side of tali, the sandhills
Mingkiri, the marsupial mouse, hides from kuniya, the desert
    python,
Miniri, the thorny devil lizard, is camouflaged in red and yellow
while irilpi, the morning dew, provides precious drops of
    kapi, water.

From wanma warara, a distant range of purple hills,
karu, the river bed, holds the twisting arms of apara, the red gums.
Wanampi, the giant Rainbow Serpent, carved the features of the landscape
but in the time of storms and flooded tjukula, beware his presence in deep water.

Ngintaka, the Perentie Lizard Man, dislikes the yellow splotches on his back.
He searches for Milpali, the sand goanna, hidden in a ngati, hollow.
This is their ngura, their dwelling place, and here are their sacred sites
where all the landmarks denote their passing and tell of ancient rites.

Papa Kutjara Tjukurpa – the lands of the Two Dogs Dreaming.
Malu ngura Tjukuritja – the places of the Red Kangaroo.
Here is their kurun, their soul, their spirit, part of the manta, the land
here kana, life and Law have meaning and everything is defined.

Maku, the white witchetty grub, lives in the roots of ilykuwarra, the acacia.
Tjala, the orange honey ants, are found in nests deep under wintalyka, the mulga.
All have their Tjukur Dreaming, Law, all their place and purpose;
everything has its kanyini, its life and death connection.

Kamaralpa Tjukurpa tells of time when ice covered the land,
of Wampurrkutjara, songs of a great flood, and the coming of
   the White man –
Ngura, Tjukur, Walytja-piti Place, Dreaming and family bonds.
Rawa, tirtu, irtiringi – always, continuously, forever.

Civilisations rise and fall, but the Anangu, the people, remain.
Cultures, languages, come and go, but the inma, songs, are
   still the same.
Kana arangka, life as it was, for so long did not change
but the Walypala, the Whitefellas, came and broke the Law
   to satisfy greed and gain.

Mungartji, in the late afternoon, ngangkali, the storm clouds,
   appear.
Ailuru pulka, drought, and famine, kuli, herald a long hot
   year.
Many kuka, animals, will soon die; kaanka, the crow, waits so
   patiently.
Kapi, rain, will return life to the land and tjulpun-tjulpun
   make a floral sea.

The Piranpa, Whites, destroyed the land, bringing sickness
   and despair.
Global warming in the Lands and miil-miilpa, the sacred
   sites, were ignored.
The breakdown of the Tjukur, Law, led to many an abuse.
The tjukurtjara, missionaries, introduced their God, but not
   all practised what they preached.

Tjintungka, when the sun rises again, the Anangu will be
 wankarri, alive, once more.
Mara ala ngangkari, the healing hands of the desert doctors,
 will restore life's balance.
The power of forty thousand years or more will vanquish
 mamu, the evil spirits.
Their kurun, spirit, will soar like walawuru, the eagle, above
 their beloved manta.

Kututu kalypa, Ananguku mukulya ngaltunytju;
the heart will become peaceful, the people loving and
 compassionate.
The tarapula, the troubles of the past, will be overcome
and the dark eyes of the tjitji, children, will sparkle like the
 kililpi, stars in the Tjukal, the glorious Milky Way.

Tjintu Irititja – A Day Long Ago

Manta ngalya uturingu,
the first light of the desert dawn,
creeps like a kukaputja, a skilled hunter
forming on the horizon ilkari kantily, a glowing yellow rib.

Tjintu untantunu katji,
the sun's golden spears,
chase away the Waparitja, the Dreaming Spirits,
that dwell in the munga, the shrinking night sky.

Puyu nyaranyi, a small column of smoke,
stands above the peaceful ngura, camp,
where the Anangu, the People, wangkaringanyi, awaken
on a cool morning in piriyakutu, spring.

Apara, the red gums, like wati ngaranyi, standing guards,
munu karu kanyinyi, protect all in the sandy river bed.
para yanyanyi mantangka, the river winds across the land
like a Wanampi pulka, a giant Rainbow Snake.

Kaanka the crows are deep in mungawinki wankanyi,
    morning conversations.
Kutjara piyar-piyar, a pair of galahs, greet the new day
and over the tjukula, waterhole, kiilyi-kiilykari, the budgerigars,
flash brilliant green against ilkari, the clear blue sky.

Wangka kulini, voices, sound in the ngura, camp.
Waltjapiti pakani, family groups, emerge from their wiltja,
    shelters.
The tjitji, children, eat yesterday's roast maku, witchetty grubs,
while the kungka, women, collect waru, the firewood.

Punti, a ngunytju, mother, of the Western Desert people
tjina yananyi, walks, with Djibilla, her tjitji matja, her little girl.
In a wira, wooden dish, they collect wanguru, the grass seeds,
and their tjungari, round millstone, will grind flour for a cake.

'Ngunytju, mother! Ngunytju, malatja! Mother aunty!'
calls Djibilla ila ngura, near the camp.
'Ngayuku tjina pika, my foot is hurt.
I fell collecting mai apurama, the sweet gum leaf scale.'

'Tjitja-matja, my little girl, soon you'll be karalyarinyi, better.
Put on the mangata-quandong kuuti latja, kernel paste.
Paku wiyaringanyi, have a rest here with me
while I pauraru wantinyi, prepare to bake the seed damper.'

'Ngunytju, mother,' asks the titji, child,
'when will you do nyanpinyi, the women's dance?
And when will mama father, ngalya kulpanyi, return to camp?
And will he bring malu, the red kangaroo?'

'Tjintungka, tomorrow, we will dance
and mama father will return kuwaripa, soon.
We will all intjanma, share, the kuka, meat,
and you can eat muturrka, the kangaroo tail.'

Djibilla's kuru maru, dark eyes, twinkle.
The tjitji, children, will be pukularinyi, happy
and munganka, at night, Djibilla will pilu-pilu, fall asleep,
listening to stories of the Kungkarangkulpa, the Seven Sisters
   Dreaming.

Waru kampanyi, the coals of the campfire, glow
warming a mother and child as they kunkun ngarinyi, lie
 asleep.
Iritinguru, a long time ago, life as it always was;
but in the future ilanyi, tears, will fall, for the lost tjitji,
 children.

Kuur kuur, the night owl, sends out a warning.
Palatja! Palatja! Look out! Look out!
The Anangu, the people, sleep like miri-tjuta, the ancestors,
but soon their world will wiyaringu, come to a sudden end.

Kapi Wiya – Without Water

Kapi wiya, tjukula wiya.
Without rain, there are no waterholes.
Kapi wiya, punu wiya
Without water, there are no plants.
Punu wiya, apara wiya.
Without plants and trees, there are no river gums.
Tjulpan-tjulpan wiya, pinta-pinta wiya.
Without flowers, there are no butterflies.
Kalka wiya, wangunu wiya.
Without seeds, there are no grains.
Mai wiya, mangata wiya.
Without fruits, there are no quandongs.
Tjulpu wiya, kalaya wiya.
Without birds, there are no emus.
Kuka wiya, malu wiya.
Without animals, there are no kangaroos.
Wapar wiyaringanyi, malu wiyaringanyi
Without the Creation Time, kangaroos do not exist.
Anangu wiya, Wapar wiya.
Without the people, there is no Dreaming.
Yuru wiya, Tjunguringanyi wiya.
Without life's fluids, there is no joining together.
Kurun wiya, walytjapiti wiya.
Without the spirit of life, there are no family bonds.
Kapingku kana kanyini.
Water connects all life.

Tracks and Trails of the Centre

Along ancient tracks
Ediacaran fossils
tell of life
in the beginning.

Marine reptiles swam
in the Eromanga Sea
while giant turtles
left prints on the sand.

Wanampi
the powerful Rainbow Snake
carved the landscape
in the Dreaming.

The Ancestral Beings
moved over the land,
their trails and creations
defining the world.

For millennia the people
of the Centre
followed secret routes
between sources of water.

Expert eyes
read the soil for signs
of animal tracks
and friend or foe.

In 1860
the explorer Stuart
gave new names
to the Centre lands.

Twelve years later
the telegraph line
crossed the continent –
a message highway.

Bullock wagons
and camel trains
scored the earth
with dusty scars.

Cattle and horses
camels and goats
covered the tracks
of the native animals.

Metal rails
traversed red sand
bringing White masters
and their workers.

The boots of White men
led to camps
where barefooted Black women
conceived Black/White babies.

Mounted police
and T-model Fords
rounded up children
leaving a trail of tears.

February the thirteenth
2008
Reconciliation paths
all lead to Canberra

The 'Sorry' apology
helped heal some pain
but the future road
is still unknown.

2

European Settlement: the Coming of the Piranpa, White People

The Saga of Squatter John

1. Birth: Yorkshire, UK, 1857

Blue woodsmoke rises above Silton Grange farm;
rain and mist cover the grey stone walls.
The harvest is done and the elm's patches of gold
herald the beginning of autumn and the summer's fall.

1857, and in late September
a christening for John, born to Elizabeth Bailes,
and proud father William the 'gentleman farmer'
readies the horses to cross the Dales.

Summer. Autumn. Winter. Spring.
The seasons come and the seasons go.
The buttercups sway in the lush green fields,
and the North York moors are covered in snow.

From boarding school young scholar John was sent
home for the harvest and hard work with Pa.
Education was the future – engineering a good trade
which would take John away, to a life afar.

Factories and smoke, pressure on land and city;
industrial England fed on a mighty empire.
'Go forth, young man! Seek your fortune!' was the cry.
John was unafraid, to South Australia he would aspire.

2. Arrival in Australia, 1880s

From Fowler's Bay on horse and camel, across Wirangu lands,
across Sturt's Stony Desert, across the Simpson's sands,
John sank bores for precious water – the Dreamtime was no more.
Farmers' dreams crushed Native Title; all that remained was
    White Man's law.

Living on the Parade in Norwood, in 1885
John met Mary Hynes, with her pretty auburn hair.
Soon they were married at St Bartholemew's
and within two years, baby Frank was in their care.

More government contracts, in the Flinders and beyond;
family in a tent on the Nullarbor Plain.
Searing heat in summer made life hard for mother Mary,
but soon the hand of fate would cause her even greater pain.

The 'Null-arbor', the 'treeless' desert
supported life for those who knew
how to find the bluebush berries,
how to eat ripe quandongs too.

There grew a tree, in the 'treeless' desert;
a quandong struggled to live, and flower alone,
and three-year-old Frank took the fruit the desert peach offered,
not knowing death waited in the quandong's stone.

A few months later, John's brother Cooper
arrived from the West, where the sandalwood price
had collapsed, leaving many fortune hunters
without work and living on the roll of a dice.

Life was simple at bore number four.
Young brother Cooper had much to gain
and when the dust washed from their faces
whisky dulled their senses and their pain.

Another year later and new baby Stella
would give Mary some comfort while living alone.
John in the desert and Mary in Adelaide –
a family apart, an empty bed in the home.

3. Home to England

1892 and all are home to England.
John's brother Frank is on the farm, now in Leicestershire.
Their father William's still at work, despite advancing years,
and Ma is glad to see her family, and have them 'over here'.

July in England, green woods and yellow wheat fields,
narrow roads cross stone bridges where quiet waters flow.
Who in their right mind would leave all this beauty?
But John, ever practical, knew to Australia he must go.

John and baby Stella, along with a very pregnant Mary,
had planned to board in London, a cabman all prepaid,
but Mary was too ill to travel and boarding was not possible
until they travelled on to Plymouth, where their journey
   could be made.

The ship would stop first at Gibraltar,
then on to Naples, with its famous bay,
past the pyramids and Egypt's antiquities,
John with baby Stella, Mary sick on many a day.

The Red Sea was calm, the Indian Ocean heaved.
The steamship *Orizaba* continued 'cross the sea.
At last land loomed large before them
and, out of Albany, a newborn son would please.

4. Colony, SA Far North/Central Australia

Would baby William 'Orizaba' Bailes
restore Mary's spirit and drive away the pain
that drove her to take the whisky bottle,
when others slept, or worked again?

John could not leave her, with all her problems,
not for a day, not for a week.
John took all four deep into the outback,
where he opened a general store, located at Bloods Creek.

There he met the camel trains
bound for the Alice, some days away
There he traded, in the rare desert skins
of marsupial moles, which gave good pay.

1895, and another baby, Cooper,
was born, down south, to John and wife.
Mary was better (or so it seemed)
and returned up north for the pioneer's life.

Two years later and Mary, thirty-six,
looked after three children and helped John run the store.
John still went boring; his skill was well known;
a silver derrick stood on the shelf, a gift from years before.

And so another contract, perhaps a final journey
to drill again for water, in the southern Arrernte lands.
Metal bits and casings would pierce the desert's body
until ancient artesian water came flooding through the sands.

It was a final journey; the spirit world beckoned Mary
across the sweeping desert, across the purple range.
The heat haze shimmered in the distance, creating strange
　illusions.
Who was coming here for Mary? Whose god lived in this
　land so strange?

Night time in the desert, a quiet time in the desert.
White men would sleep, while desert animals looked for prey.
Mary fed her little children in the confines of the tent
and readied them for bed, an oil lamp showing them the way.

Was it a baby's sudden motion? Was it the dingoes' distant
　howling?
But the oil lamp would fall and fill the tent with flames.
Mary saved her precious children and John put out the fire
but the badly burned mother would die, mumbling all their
　names.

John hid his inner sadness his children needed care.
He turned to the desert mothers, no white nursemaids here.
A widow from Macumba, Louise, came to stay;
a 'housekeeper' was her title, they soon became a 'pair'.

5. 1900, Federation and Federal Station

A vast lease of land, from the Crown,
would give John 'rights' to a fait accompli;
the turn of the century, the turn of the White man,
forty thousand years gone, all without a plea…

Talk of Federation was rife across the nation,
British or Australian, a colony no more.
John showed his true allegiance, or was it a sense of humour,
when he named his station Federal, before the change of law?

Luritja and Arrernte, Wongkanguru and Dieri
living in two worlds, the Black and the White.
The women no longer naked, messages from missions,
the hunters now on horses, with cattle day and night.

Early 1900s and the Federation drought
halved the cattle numbers, leaving skin and bone and flies.
Huge dust storms from the desert arose in giant waves
with their red and orange dust, blotting out blue skies.

Green coolabah gums line Possum Creek,
the evening sky burns like a fire.
John watches as orange turns to deep red;
what must he do to survive nature's ire?

The traditional owners worked with the land –
a fine tuned balance, devoid of abuse.
Now John would buy angora goats;
two thousand roamed – would they be of use?

Day upon day, year after year.
Would the rains come? Would clouds appear?
The sleeping seeds in the desert waited patiently,
until the crash of thunder and the lightning's spear.

The cutting red dust, speckled with silver mica
creeps, then rushes across the broad plains,
but this time the heavens open, allowing new hoping;
will the roof be coping, with all this heavy rain?

The drought has finally broken, the land will live anew,
the purple parakilya flowers, the desert daisies bloom;
soft yellows, pinks, mauves and whites
transform the barren desert, expelling all the gloom.

Camels and horses, cattle and goats,
now John can restock, with the grasses' growth so high.
With water from bores and cool tanks on the house
John had fruit, flowers and vegetables, for many passers-by.

In the far north of South Australia, in the middle of the desert,
Padre Ploughman came to visit the fabled garden green.
Along the bottle pathways, lined with flowers, trees and colour
he supped with John and Louise and marvelled at the scene.

Famed for her healing, many came to see Louise;
it was said she worked wonders and cured all disease,
and if a bushman had toothache, John the engineer
would remove the painful problem with relative ease.

Another time the padre was asked to assist
'Old Man John' with bush races, to outwit a cad
who came from down south – simple bushmen to fleece
with lies and lame horses – caught out, he left sad.

1915 and another deadly drought
slowly strangles the land, the cattle it kills,
while away from Australia our young soldiers die
on the beaches at Gallipoli and in the Turkish hills.

The Great War is over, the Anzacs come home,
thousands dead in the trenches, many maimed too.
'Welcome home, digger.' The crowd wave their flags
but another angel of death comes as the Spanish flu.

On the edge of the Witjira, John shares the lands
with the last of the Arrernte, as they gather and plan
their last great corroborees, the last gathering of clans
in the far distant places of the once hidden inland.

The land is under pressure, the old ways are no more.
Gone are the traditional tracks, gone are the traditional foods,
massacres and missionaries; all kill in their own way.
The Spanish flu takes from the whites, but decimates the blacks.

'Old Man John' or 'Arthur', John had his outback names.
His home brew drunk from pewter pots
was known to all, and travelling guests
enjoyed time with him, though his bladder did not!

In 1920, John and Louise
stayed with the Johannsens at Deep Well.
They had arrived by camel buggy, and to young Kurt it was quite funny
when they could only eat their meat with the aid of a mincing mill.

Soon Cooper and Bill ran the station and store;
John and Louise were in poor health.
The healing waters and herbs at Dalhousie Springs
were ignored by Whites, with their doctors and wealth.

6. Death and the Future – the Ruins in the Witjira

John lost Louise in 1922.
To Adelaide he retired, where daughter Stella
nursed the old pioneer, the well borer and squatter,
and listened to his stories and to what he would tell her.

November the ninth, three years later,
John's life at an end, he'd meet his Maker.
The North Road Cemetery saw his body at rest
but his spirit would fly back to the red lands of the Centre.

His niece Bette would recall how he gave her a sweet.
Daughter Stella moved south to a home far away.
Sons Bill and Cooper battled floods, drought and heat,
while brother Cooper remembered the hard work and hard play.

John was long dead, when a grandson was born
to a 'White' father Cooper and 'Black' mother Mary;
a link to the past, a life in the present,
hope for a future, no longer contrary.

Crow talks to crow in the cool of the morning;
pink and grey galahs screech over Bloods Creek.
The Ancestral Spirits and John are here in the desert,
where time is not measured by days in the week.

Red sand blows over the yellow stone walls.
The wind whispers in ruins, where once there was meaning.
The fruit trees and vines have long since gone
from the land of the perentie, from the Great Lizard Dreaming.

The Ballad of Old Bill

In Alice Springs, a stone memorial,
erected by 'his old bush mates',
marks the last resting place
of Old Bill.

Old Bill
could tell a story – and many a story
was told of the man with the many names
from the Red Centre lands.

William O. Bailes
was born on a ship – or in the harbour;
son of squatter John – whose sense of humour
gave Bill the second name 'Orizaba'.

Red-haired Rudd
would lose his mother – after a fire in a tent.
Black northern mothers would give him comfort,
and White Louise – 'the Mother of the North'.

Young schoolboy Bill
was sent to St Peter's
dressed in a tie and a college cap,
a world away from the stockman's boots and the drover's hat.

'Aba Bailes (or was it Harbour?)
grew up in the outback – riding a horse
where the sound of crows and cattle whips
echoed in the dusty heat.

Outback race meets at Bloods Creek,
run by Old Man John, went for a week
and all the bushmen of the north
would gather to gamble and test their worth.

Bill, along with brother Cooper,
would drove their cattle along many tracks
down south to Adelaide and across the border
through the many hardships of the harsh outback.

In Adelaide, Bill bought a car,
a Ford model T, straight from the dealer.
No licence, nor lessons, he drove it far
with the handbrake on, his new four-wheeler!

Another time he bought a boat
but drought decreed it would not float
until a flood many years later
but the white ants were first – their need was greater!

At the end of the war to end all wars,
Bill married Faye and their children came.
They lived in Adelaide – Bill worked on cars
but the outback called and Bill could not stay.

A man of his times, Bill could turn his magic hands
to divine water for bores, or fence the land.
Fix engines, run goats, corral cattle for brands,
try camel partnerships, till rails crossed the sand.

White men living in a Black man's land,
Perentie Dreaming and dreams of gold.
Lasseter lost, in the sacred places
White men, Black women and coloured faces.

The desert nights have wondrous sights –
the blood-red sunsets, the brilliant stars.
A man can be cold, the Aboriginal women shy,
but Bill kept warm and with them did lie.

Bill's brother Cooper lived with two Desert sisters.
A child with each – young Billy and June –
but Bill's seed fell both near and far;
tiny bones would gleam in the light of the moon.

At night the camp fires crackled and burned.
The outback men came from many a mile
to drink whisky and tell the tall stories
of poisonous weeds, murder, drought and doubtful glories.

Cooper, a former buckjump champ and breaker,
would drink with Bill, who seemed quite sober
until his mates would put him on his horse
and homeward bound it would take its course.

Ron 'Pulla' Smith from New Crown was able
to arrange a meeting for widower Bill, with Mabel.
At Eringa station an outback wedding day
would see Cooper and Billy give Rudd away.

The Bailes brothers and their kith and kin
would run the store at Abminga siding.
Cousin John, passing through on the Ghan, would give a grin
to recognise lost family, at such a place residing.

October, sixty-five, in the Old Timers' Home,
Bill seemed fine and the sun was hot;
early he watered the red geranium pot
and around the home he tidied up.

In an ancient land the spirits are near;
what would Bill have need to fear?
He lay down carefully on the bed,
and when Mabel found him, he was dead.

While many would mourn an old pioneer
and his mates would recall him over a beer,
his family and children had mixed emotion
for he'd let them drift as in the ocean.

He was not always there when needed most
but Mabel would shed a tear for her man
and the jokers would say the stones on the grave
would keep old Bill in and the women safe.

But I recall the preacher's words
about casting the first stones – for all have sinned
and now the bones of Black and White
return to dust from whence they came.

Old Bill could talk and tell a tale.
In many relationships he would fail,
but Billy recalls how they'd laugh and joke,
'Old Rudd, he was a good old bloke.'

Love Story from the Lands of Ngintaka

Ted Lennon was as hardy as a mulga post
and had grown up in the remote outback
where he was respected as a top drover
with an Irishman's love of whiskey and women.

In the 1920s Ted visited Bloods Creek
where the Bailes brothers ran a pub and station
and here he would drink with his good mate Cooper
and sleep with Indurkuta – the Desert Rose.

Rose was a daughter of the Western Desert people
with dark brown eyes and light brown hair
and had lived her young life in the lands of Ngintaka
working hard as the Bailes' goatherd girl.

Rose had an independent mind and spirit
that flew in the face of the old traditions
but unafraid she watched and waited
for the strong arms of her blue-eyed lover.

Ted would come back from long cattle drives
and return to see Rose and their daughter Molly
but old Charlie Maramuku with the 'clever hands'
wanted Indurkuta for his youngest wife.

Jealous Charlie had taken young Molly
past a secret inma performed by men
and for this breaking of the Tjukur, Law,
someone in her family must surely die.

One cold dark winter's night in late July
Rose and Molly slept under sheltering branches
next to their campfire's glowing red coals
beneath the brilliant pathway of the desert stars.

Like a hunter, Charlie sneaked up to their *wiltja*
and set fire to the dry apara leaves
but Rose was able to save young Molly
even though she'd received fatal burns.

When Ted returned and asked for Rose,
old Charlie said that she had died,
and with that news the tough bearded bushman
put his head in his hands and quietly cried.

Ted told Charlie Maramuku
to take Molly to the Bailes' homestead
where Aba's wife Faye would give her care
but cunning Charlie had other plans in mind.

The next day Molly was playing with little Mary
when Molly's aunt tricked Mary to leave
and quickly hid her niece in their wagon
and left Bloods Creek for another life.

Many years later Ted and Cooper
would meet together and drink for days
and Ted recalled the death of old Charlie
who had mysteriously 'drowned' in a waterhole.

Ngintaka the Perentie Lizard Man
had created the lands for his people
and in times of reflection Ted would grieve
for the lost daughters of old Ngintaka.

Simpson Desert Crossing, 1936

Ted Colson was as strong as a bullock –
an outback character with many talents,
a bushman, explorer, writer and scholar,
a storyteller with a sense of humour.

When not away on his adventures
Ted ran Bloods Creek store and station.
He'd taken over from Cooper Bailes
a neighbour on Federal and on Eringa.

Living on the edge of the Simpson Desert
there was a challenge for a man like Ted.
No one had crossed this part of the Centre.
'It couldn't be done,' many had said.

But in early thirty-six, breaking rains
gave Ted a chance to make a crossing.
He carefully prepared for an arduous mission
asking 'Eringa' Peter to be his partner.

Lean and wiry Peter Haines
was a quiet Western Desert stockman –
a 'smart bloke' with a tracker's eye,
in a harsh environment he could survive.

Constable Kennett from Charlotte Waters
had come to farewell Ted and Peter –
his official inspection hardly needed
for a family friend and bushman like Ted.

Ted said goodbye to the grieving constable,
remembering his mate's recent misfortune
when his two young daughters, Rosslyn and Joyce,
had lost their lives to choking diphtheria.

The twenty-sixth of May in that year
saw Ted and Peter leave Bloods Creek.
They took food and water for many weeks
with only a compass to show the way.

Over high red dunes and yellow salt flats
the two men on camel rode to the east.
Rain had transformed a once arid land
with grasses, flowers and newly formed lakes.

At night around a long-burning fire
Ted and Peter talked about their lives
and Ted would use the desert words
to talk of the Dreaming and its laws.

Ted named some hills after Alice his wife.
So many times she'd been left alone
they were without children, but Ted had a son
born to a dark daughter of the Centre.

Eringa Peter had left his wife Mary
back at their camp next to Bloods Creek.
She'd been angry and resentful when he left
to risk his life for a White man's plan.

After many days and countless sand dunes
Ted and Peter ascended a steep rising ridge
and there below lay a flooded valley
full of daisies, desert pea and yellow wattle.

Kangaroos, emus and feral camels
grazed on the grasses next to the lakes.
Freckled duck, crimson chats and flocks of pelicans
lived in a lost world in a fleeting paradise.

Ted gazed in awe at this verdant scene
and remembered the recent death of Joyce
with her golden curls just like the wattle
and sparkling eyes like the sun on blue water.

The flood out of the Todd and Hale rivers
was here deep in the Simpson Desert.
Glen Joyce, the name Ted gave the valley
to remember a girl whose laugh was gone.

Some days later, Ted and Peter arrived
at the Birdsville pub where local patrons
were surprised two men had made such a journey
with minimal fuss and no fanfare.

Ted took everything in his stride.
After two days he said to Peter,
'I suppose we'd better make a move
back to our wives and to our homes.'

Cooper the Cattleman (1895–1963)

1. Old Timers' Home, Alice Springs, Central Australia

As they say in the bush, he was tall for his height,
and his legs were bowed from hard life on the 'Run'.
Old Cooper's yellow eyes squint in the light
like an old goanna, half asleep in the sun.

He stands in the doorway of the Old Timers' Home
on a hot Sunday in November 1963.
He shakes my hand, but his strength has all but gone
and his life will soon fade, like the smoke on the breeze.

The olive-green oleander adorned with red flowers
casts broken shadows across the white gravel path.
The soft pinks, mauves and browns of the majestic
   MacDonnell Ranges
rise up from the orange sands of the desert's dusty bath.

Cooper mumbles a few brief words of greeting.
Overhead the ring neck parrots screech and fly
from de Fontenay's date farm, where pleasant eating
was disturbed by a gunshot – and a farmer's cry.

Cooper's eyes have a faraway look, a strangeness;
what is the sadness that lies deep inside?
He is here but his spirit strains at the harness
like his favourite horse ready for the ride…

Twenty-fifth of November, Cooper ceases to breathe
'No, he never married,' said sad brother Bill,
but deep in the desert a son of the Arrernte and Luritja
would return to the Alice, a father to grieve.

2. Federal Station, Far North of SA, Early Life

Cooper was born in Adelaide, in 1895,
his father John, a well borer, a respected engineer.
Troubled mother Mary mourned a son, no longer alive,
not knowing fire in the desert would take her within two years.

Two-year-old Cooper, along with Bill and Stella,
was left without a mother in a harsh, strange terrain.
Now their small white arms would cling to the Arrernte women
and these early memories for Cooper would always remain.

Father John would prosper, with a store, pub and station
well-known at Bloods Creek and the Federal run.
His two sons from the Centre were sent south to St Peter's
where their 'education' was completed, with very little fun.

Back to the far north, back to the Red Centre
Cooper worked the station, a rider of note.
A man who knew cattle, how to work the land,
this was where he belonged, this life had his vote.

Many years later and I am reading the newspaper.
The 'Fifty-years ago' column catches my eye
for there it mentions Cooper as the SA buckjump champion –
a dangerous occupation when the wild hooves fly!

His father, the 'Squatter', died late in '25.
Cooper continued on, working with Black and White
but Federal station struggled to keep the cattle alive
where once the people of the desert gave the land respite.

The heat would not defeat you, the flies and dust would greet you,
the lack of feed would squeeze you, but if the bores ran dry
and if the long drought could not be broken
there was no more hoping and all that was left was to watch your animals die.

The last of the cattle are taken, before drought and death overcome them
across the painted deserts, around the gleaming white salt pans.
The ancient tracks were once trodden with care by the desert peoples
but now are trampled into oblivion, by the herds of the worried White man.

A station abandoned here, a cattleman struggling there,
Cooper walked from Federal Station, with his horse and a camel or two.
One man's misfortune is another's opportunity
as Kidman's empire swallowed up the properties of the unlucky few.

3. Eringa Station, Far North of SA, Cooper and Mary

So Cooper came to Eringa, cattle and horses he knew so well.
He'd work for Sir Sidney Kidman, a manager in the making.
The sun would not set on the far-flung British Empire
and bigger than England were the properties of the 'Cattle King'.

In the centre of Australia, the Arrernte and Luritja
had never heard of 'titles', and what was 'Crown lease' land?
They lived here in the desert, the desert lived in them.
Their land was bought and sold. How could they understand?

Mary Nyukabinna, sometimes known as Mary Cleanskin,
came from Southern Arrernte land in time of dire need.
Measles and influenza, drought and desperate hunger
reduced life in the desert with a frightening, deadly speed.

The old kinship system shattered – no mothers for the children.
The missions offered help, in their White Christian ways.
Heaven in the future, salvation in the present.
Many thanked a white saviour – the generous Mary Hayes.

And so Mary came to Eringa, living in a creek bed,
soft sand for a floor, tin and branches overhead.
Gidgee fire in winter, kangaroo dogs for extra warmth,
bush tucker from the desert, flour and beef when Cooper said.

A young woman of the Centre, a mature White man on the station:
the laws of nature do not discriminate between Black and White.
The hunter and provider has moral responsibility
not to abuse what is given in the passion of the night.

White moonlight covers the curves of the bare stone hills,
white bodies press against black breasts, thighs and faces.
The windmill's shaft rises and falls in the warm night breeze
and the waters of life seep from all the secret places.

Cooper and Mary had an understanding, not just of Desert culture,
for theirs was a bond between two equal mates.
The law forbade 'physical relations'– but when dark eyes and hands beckoned,
Cooper followed Mary and in the river's bed their love they'd consummate.

Cooper and Mary had grown up in the desert.
In their own way they have belonged here and to one another.
No gold wedding rings, no idealised Western romance,
no bedrooms with en suite, just life on the land together.

Sometime in '37, Mary was pregnant
and a baby Billy Bailes was born at Eringa.
Named after Cooper's brother William, the once carefree 'coloured' baby
would soon sense the fears of the 'Stolen Generations'.

World War Two dragged on, many miles away –
a struggle with the Nazis and Imperial Japanese.
Australia's beef cattle supported civilian and soldier
with bully beef at the front; at home, rations and tinned peas.

1946, Cooper still manages Eringa
and coming from down south is young 'new chum' Bruce Delany.
Life here was very basic: no electricity, engines, phones,
contact with 'civilisation' by horse and camel buggy.

A raw youth from the city, Bruce would learn very quickly
how to ride a horse and muster bullocks at full speed.
How to cook a decent damper, how to tell a mopoke from a parrot,
how to rely on mates, how to find water when there was need.

The coloured Marilyn Monroes giggle, their unkempt hair in a straggle.
Loose clothes barely conceal bare bodies and sex is in the air.
The stockmen of any colour vie for their favours and attentions
giving them cheap presents, for flowers don't grow here!

Ride the wild horses! The women if you dare!
The strong legs of the stockmen entwine with smooth dark skin.
The law of Luritja and Arrernte allows take and give.
Bodies locked together are nature, but abuse and force is sin.

Cooper would tell Bruce stories of bush pubs, goats and
   'characters'
sitting around a campfire, under a coolabah tree.
Bruce would listen, and later wonder how his boss managed
   not to go under
when with Ted Lennon they drank neat rum together, or
   mixed it with tea!

Never far away was Cooper's brother, called 'Aba', 'Rudd' or
   'Bill'
he'd visit at the station and tell a tale or two.
A family left in Adelaide, he was married to the bush
the spell of the outback bound him, there was nothing he
   could do.

One day at Oodnadatta, Bill was in a fight –
pretty normal in the Outback, a fairly common sight.
But Bill upset too many: Ernie Kempe called for a fine
for being 'drunk and disorderly'; Ernie had a plan in mind.

He'd fine Rudd five pounds, but reduce it down to one,
but when Bill heard the sentence, in temper he would call
'I bloody well won't pay it!' So Ernie reluctantly
let the five pounds stand, to the amusement of nearly all.

Bruce soon moved down to Macumba, now a seasoned ringer.
Kidmans used Eringa for new men their trade to make.
Many years later, when George Birchmore managed Macumba
he told Bruce the famous story of Cooper and the snake.

A poisonous preserved snake, in a round glass jar.
A surprised visitor Frank, hears Cooper talking, as if at a bar.
'Mister Snake, I need this spirit much more than you!'
The lid is removed and all the murky contents too!

During World War Two, Cooper went down south
to buy up supplies for Eringa Station.
While on the long journey home on the Old Ghan,
Cooper decided to sample the tempting whiskey ration.

The train was full of soldiers on their way to Darwin.
One was young John Kempe, the son of old Ernie.
When the train was derailed, someone said to John,
'There's a passenger Cooper Bailes trapped in the roll over.'

John knew Cooper well from earlier Kidman meetings
and quickly went to see if Cooper needed help.
When he found Cooper asleep after hours of drinking,
he carefully woke him saying, 'Cooper, there's been an accident.'

As Cooper came to and heard young John speak
he became a little concerned and asked John in surprise,
'Where's the accident, John?' 'What do we need to do?'
John said, 'Just follow me,' as a smile flickered in his eyes.

Another time on Eringa, Cooper and brother Bill were on a muster
and with a thirsty herd of cattle Bill went to test the depth of nearby water.
'It's ball high, Cooper,' he called to his much taller brother
who replied, 'In that case, Bill, we'd better move the herd a little further.'

The bushmen were hard drinkers and some women held their own.
Binge drinking was quite common, the scourge of many a home.
when Cooper hit the whisky bottle, throw away the cork;
bouts of alcoholism would hasten an end to cattle work.

4. Abminga Siding, the Ghan Railway, Far North of SA

The early 1950s would see Cooper, along with Rudd,
working at Abminga siding, managing the store.
For wanderers in the desert, for visitors on the Ghan,
here lived the Bailes brothers with their women and a few more.

Cooper taught young Billy about cattle and showed him how to ride.
Billy disappeared on a camel when Welfare were abroad.
Other times Cooper argued with them, a gun at his side.
He'd lost his mother early; he'd protect Billy from the Protection Board.

Mary's younger sister Daisy, an aunt or mother to Billy
gave birth to Cooper's daughter June – no great scandal here.
It was the Arrernte way, consensus suited all,
but alcohol weakened the protection for a little 'half-caste' girl.

Taken from her mother's arms to 'a better life',
June was sent away, down south, to distant Adelaide.
Colebrook Home awaited her – later, foster-parents came
and so her ties to her past were severed with much pain.

1959 and Billy's gone to Macumba
working for George Birchmore, Cooper's old mate.
Another Bailes family, cousin John, wife Marj and children,
would stop briefly at Abminga as the Ghan left the state.

A year or two later, Cooper, Bill and Mabel
would retire to the Alice, in the Old Timers' Home.
Out past the Gap, carved by an ancient river,
they'd spend precious time together, no fear of being alone.

At Ly Underdown's Alice Springs Hotel, Cooper came to
    meet old mates
and here there'd be memories of floods and droughts,
of cattle drives and champion rides, of poisonous snakes
and tragic fates; all this and more, they would relate.

Then late one summer's day with the sun's slanting rays,
Cooper left the hotel to find his way home.
He tripped over on a gutter and when he hit his head
the passers-by who found him, thought he was dead.

Cooper seemed to recover, but his brain found it harder
to cope with the simple life, and anything new.
Son Billy was quite furious; Ly had left his dad's life ruinous,
even though most said there was nothing anyone could do.

5. Kanyini – Connection Past, Present, Future

Sitting in a chair in the early evening,
a tough old man of the outback awaits his fate.
His eyes stare at the MacDonnell Ranges in the heart of the Centre
where they rose from the Dreamtime, before any White man's date.

Life's vitality is fading, but some images remain.
From deep within his being a spark can reignite
the memories of passion, where sweat glistens on black skin
like the rash of polished stars in the Milky Way at night.

The motion of riding on his favourite chestnut mare
cannot be forgotten, nor the places of creation
like the still blue waters of Eringa waterhole
and the untouched worlds and valleys, scattered 'cross the station.

Strehlow's beloved songs of the Arrernte may now be broken,
and Cooper had his share of guilt and shame.
Where were his family – his lover, son and daughter?
Only brother Bill and Mabel could guess at his pain.

Cooper's eyes moisten over and not from the wind
but from the deep well of emotion that lies deep within.
Rudd's 'beloved brother' would be 'ever-remembered'
and the love of son Billy would always stay with him.

The gidgee camp fire burns brightly through the night.
The Ancestor Beings patrol the heights.
The God of the desert will soon welcome a lost soul
for Cooper's spirit will soon be in flight.

Uluru, Ayers Rock, Uluru once again.
Kata Tjuta, the Olgas, the many heads of the Dreaming.
Federal, Eringa and Abminga are all gone now
but among us, and in them, are our creator beings.

And here I am standing, a tear in my eye.
Old Cooper is gone but baby Matthew is born.
Life turns a full circle and death is no more.
Tjukurrpa. Karma. Transcendence. Salvation.

Bush Christmas, circa 1930

Puffs of orange dust rise and fall
to the rhythm of the horses' hooves.
The weary stockmen hurry homeward, racing the failing light.

Low in a pale blue sky, the white fire of the evening star
heralds their arrival.
The long arms of the river gums are silhouetted against blood
    red skies
and in the creek bed, the Black Madonnas sing Dreamtime songs
to hush their holy infants' cries.

Three men alight from their mounts, their faces streaked with
    grime.
The cattle troughs bring wet relief, the men are home in time.
Barefoot children, with bright eyes, shout excitedly,
'How was the muster?' 'Did you see old Bill?' 'Anything from
    the store for me?'
'You'll have to wait till tomorrow when it's Christmas Day.'
The men tend to their horses and put their gear away.

Fresh beef from the station, cooked on an open fire,
fills empty stomachs as the men talk of past Christmas Eves.
Some drink black billy tea for their thirst and some whisky
    for release.
Cooper recalls Christmas carols and choirs of angels singing
'God and sinners reconciled' – to that he could relate.
God would not mind his lover was Black, unlike the laws of
    the state.

A light cotton dress in a brown paper bag, a gift for his
 Arrernte mate.
The warm summer's night, goodwill to all, a White man and
 a Black woman.
Two hundred yards from the homestead, to her camp he'd go.
The saltbush and bluebush lit the way – silver under a yellow
 moon.
The mass of stars a heavenly host, in a silent night,
a holy night, God's pure love, bodies created for earthly delight.

Weeks spent in the saddle, leather reins in his hands,
soon he'd be with Mary, on a blanket on the sand
'Mary,' Cooper called softly; she knew his voice so well.
'I've brought you a Christmas present, open it and see.'
Mary's eyes flash with surprise and laughter as she opens it
 gratefully.

Words whispered in Arrernte – two lovers at their ease,
both reared by Black mothers, both aware of each other's needs.
Mary flings away her faded rags – naked as the desert hills.
Cooper's eyes drink in the sight, for every curve and crevice
 thrills,
and Mary tries on her new dress, under the moon's soft light.
She has no gift to bring save her body, which will be given in
 the night.

The dress is fine, but this is not the place or time
for clothes to be on bodies.
The son of Man stands before her and she the Mother of the
    Earth –
natural in her nakedness and sex no shameful act.
There, in a rough brush shelter, lower than a cattle shed,
Cooper kneels at the holy altar of his bare Black Mary.
Man cannot live by bread alone and, without, he will not live.

The desert night is quiet under the pristine Milky Way.
Cooper and Mary Nyukabinna, side by side, are far away.
Black and White together, caught in a lover's deep, embalming
    sleep.
The Eve of Christ the Saviour – were they in His keep?
A brief moment in Eternity, an eternity of Time;
the laws of the Tjukurrpa, the visions of John the Divine.

Pale yellows and pink on the horizon chase away the stars.
Soft brown ranges emerge as the tide of night recedes.
The cacophonous calls of the crows warn Cooper he must fly
as Cooper gazes at his sleeping beauty, black breasts, back
    and thighs.
Christmas Day dawns and the corellas, like white angels in
    the sky,
celebrate life in their blue cathedral and a hope that will not die.

Accident at Eringa, 1946

Ageless river red gums line the long expanse
of the still blue waters of Eringa waterhole.

Sleek fast horses and well-fed Hereford cattle
drink from the edge of this desert oasis.

An Aboriginal youth with a wiry build
always comes to help with the working horses.

The friendly young lad is liked by all
who live and work at Eringa station.

Cooper the boss is fond of the lad
who shares with him a love of horses.

One fateful day the youth is kicked
by a startled horse and falls to the ground.

Cooper and his ringers rush to the boy
who is lying on the ground in great pain.

The boy's only hope is to get to Abminga
and from there to Finke with its new airstrip.

Abminga siding is a good hour away
over red sand hills and across stony plains.

Cooper leaves with the boy by horse and buggy
and rings Constable Brown at Finke police station.

'Come quick, Ron,' a desperate Cooper explains.
'One of our boys is hurt and in a bad way.'

Ron calls up a friend, the reliable Jack Colson,
and in Jack's Land Rover they drive to Abminga.

The badly injured youth is carefully placed
on a canvas stretcher in the rear of the Rover.

Back in Finke the boy is examined
by Constable Brown and those at the station.

No bones are broken and there is no blood,
but later in the night the youth passes away.

Finally Ron discovers a small hole in the skull
where a sharp sliver of quartz had punctured the brain.

Later, Cooper takes the boy's body back home
where Black and White can grieve together.

The cries from the sorry camp give some release
as Cooper sits on the banks of the ancient waterhole.

The quiet waters mirror an eternal crimson sunset
as a reflective Cooper sips on a glass of whiskey.

The nature and length of life remain a mystery
but here by the water's edge there is a world at peace.

Flight to the Spring of Ngintaka

Cooper the cattleman had heard the news
that the police were out searching for children
fathered by White men just like him
and born to Black women like his housemaid Mary.

Cooper hurriedly left the station homestead
and ran through red dust to Mary's place
where she lived with her extended family
and her young son Billy, loved by all.

Cooper talked to Mary in her language
and warned of the danger to young Billy
for while their son had a dark complexion,
his light brown eyes told of a White connection.

Cooper and Mary knew where to go
for there was a sacred site made in the Dreaming
where Wati Ngintaka, the Perentie Lizard Man,
created a spring with clear clean water.

Cooper saddled Cinderella, his chestnut mare,
then prepared a camel for Mary and Billy
and took a supply of food from the kitchen
so that Mary and Billy would not go hungry.

In the orange stone hills not too far away,
Billy and Mary found their place to camp
where a fire in a cave gave them warmth
and where they could hide and be out of sight.

During the day Mary trapped rabbits
and dug up tjanmata, the wild bush onions.
Then as daylight faded she stoked the fire
and cooked up bush tucker for both to share.

Billy's djamu, his grandfather Tom,
had told Billy stories of old Ngintaka
such as how Ngintaka had chased Milpali the goanna
and made life-giving waterholes throughout the land.

In the hidden places of the Eringa hills,
Ngintaka had stopped with his stolen wives
and, to confuse the vengeful Kurdaitcha men,
had made munga, the night, to enable escape.

Billy played near the cave, their home
but never too far from his mother Mary.
He climbed on the massive orange and white boulders
and helped gather mulga between scattered bluebush.

After some days, Billy's father arrived
telling his family all was clear
and Billy recalled that his hiding place
was better than a face covered in coal.

The Long Journey of Billy the Stockman

1. Genesis: Central Australia, 1900s

Booming thunder echoes along the ancient stone ranges.
Heavily pregnant storm clouds tower overhead.
Distant lighting flashes and the sun's last escaping rays
glint on the galahs' grey-white wings and on their chests,
    crimson red.

The storms of the monsoon sweep across the desert.
Heavy rain falls in the lands of the Arrernte, Luritja,
    Yankunytjatjara.
Thin silver ribbons of water fall from the muted browns of
    Uluru
and a shining purple mantle settles on the heads of Kata Tjuta.

Life as it was in the beginning, in the Dawn of all Creation.
The Rivers of Life will flow where the Rainbow Snake toiled.
Thor rings out his thunder, Frey's rain and sunshine nurture
    nature
while the Celtic water spirits move in the springs and
    waterholes.

The Laws of Nature, the Laws of the Tjukurrpa Dreaming
are here in the orange sands, pink stones and purple range,
in the white ghost gums, sharp spinifex and the desert daisies,
in the green and gold budgerigars, in the simple and the
    strange.

Gusts of wind lick along the sensuous curves of the desert dunes.
Malu, the Red Kangaroo Man, and Pundi, the Yellow Bush
 Tree Woman,
are lost in the rhythm of a lover's long embrace.
The Spirits of Life awaken in the land, swelling Pundi's
 stomach, filling her bosom.

A baby girl is born n the changing lands of the Centre.
Mary Nyukabinna, the 'Skinny girl', Mary 'Cleanskin'.
Father Tom Nunkuria, 'Without a beard', not like the elders,
the former hunter working with camels to make a new living.

Federation, and Australia has its own Parliament,
democracy and votes for White Australian males.
Western civilisation and a market-driven economy
will determine who has the land and who controls the sales.

Cleanskin Tom, late of Ernabella,
works for the White man with the Afghan cameleers.
Spear wound in the thigh, the old law still has a place.
But who will hear the stories? And for the land he fears.

Missionaries follow explorers; the telegraph and railway push
 further north.
Prospectors and well-borers dig in the secret sacred places.
Hunters with guns kill the desert animals and others,
while new laws and lawmakers bring tears to non-White faces.

Aboriginal lands are disappearing, shared by Crown and
 cattleman.
Cut down the desert acacias! Burn the gidgee stumps!
Run vast herds of cattle, watch rabbits clear the land,
but when drought approaches, ruin will be at hand.

Measles, gonorrhoea and fever, the Spanish flu of 1918,
spread like a wild bushfire through tinder dry terrain.
The land and people are weakened by the White man's ways;
hundreds dead in the desert – no resistance to the pain.

Near the SA–NT border, the Hayes family struggle to make a
 living.
Their cattle numbers are falling; all suffer as they strive.
Yet Pundi and her family rely on the kindly Mary Hayes.
When Tom the Kangaroo Man's away, they'll need food to
 stay alive.

Nearby is Federal station, run by Old Man John.
Working on the station, his youngest, Cooper Bailes,
is at home on the saddle, at ease with his men,
brought up on the Desert languages by the Central Desert
 females.

Elder brother Bill, known as Rudd or Aba Bailes,
had recently married, and ran John's store at Bloods Creek.
The store and bush pub were home to many outback stories
of goats and fights and riding feats and drinking parties that
 went for a week!

Cooper and Bill, the Bailes brothers, were never far apart.
Bill would often visit Cooper, for stories he'd love to tell
of how life was on the land, of problems for Black and White,
of how some Whites had killed some Blacks or Blacks their
 own would kill.

2. Federal and Eringa Stations, 1930s

The early 1930s and Mary's a kitchenhand
working on Federal station where Cooper is the boss.
A slim young woman, dark skin and hair, and eyes
attractive to bushman Cooper, a young body in a simple,
    faded dress.

Old Man Drought releases monstrous sandy dust storms –
all the dark oranges, reds and purples swirling in strange
    gyrations.
Cooper comes to Mary and in the hot, orange half-light
naked bodies are smoothed by the fine desert dust, in the
    heat of their emotions.

And so Mary is pregnant, in the land of the Perentie Dreaming.
Ngintaka, the Perentie Lizard Man, lifts up his regal, golden head.
Along his long body, splotches of yellow colour daubed
    quickly by Milpali.
Soon he will welcome newborn Billy, without a word being
    said.

Drought and rain – loss and gain
but a long, long, drought, will catch many out.
Cooper's cattle are all sold, the horses and camels look old.
Cooper and the family leave, for they must live and not grieve.

Sir Sidney Kidman is the Cattle King.
He knew when to buy, and when to sell.
Properties he acquired, some for a song.
His hand-picked men and managers worked so well.

Cooper and kin moved to Eringa –
a huge tract of land famed for its horses.
There Billy would grow up, in the Kidman chain;
there Cooper would teach him, in a school without courses.

Pundi was growing old, Grandfather Tom often bitter.
Uncle Charlie was rough, children hit with whips.
With the old laws and rituals broken, frustration took over.
Cattle trampled the tracks where once the Arrernte made trips.

Hard work on the land, a school of hard knocks.
The pleasures were few; Billy remembered the pain.
Still he recalled Dreaming stories, how the hot springs of
    Dalhousie
were made by the Ancestors with fire sticks in the plain.

Still a little 'wee-ai' during the Second World War,
Billy rode with Cooper and camped out at night.
Along the creek bed he saw camel bones caught in a tree
and heard other stories of the floods of '38.

Many men were away with a war to be fought.
Meat came from the stations for home and afar.
Australia's first nations now in new relations.
Black men were cheap labour and Black women sought after.

Out there in the desert, 'Barcoo rot' cursed the White men
but from the same desert, Billy ate the 'Blackfeller' bush tucker.
Tjala, the honey ants, nest deep under the mulga.
Maku, the white grubs, in the roots of acacia.

The old tjilpi showed him the different animal tracks
and how the greener grass grew, over hidden water.
Pundi and Mary collected the munyeroo, flower seeds,
and together they ate bush damper, sometimes with roast
    goanna.

Father Cooper had lost his mother and brother at an early age –
no recognition in 'White Australia' for a common-law Black
    'wife'.
Welfare and police would take 'half-caste' babies away –
the threat of loss for Cooper and Mary, a real fear in young
    Billy's life.

Charcoal from the campfire would blacken many a face.
The bush telegraph would tell you if danger was at hand.
A quick pair of legs, a handy horse with lively pace
or travel on a camel, to hide at a waterhole inland.

So young Billy 'grew im up' in the world of Black and White –
a more than useful cattle hand, a rider with all the tricks;
all the White man's ways he'd learnt so very well –
they'd serve him now and in the future, when in their world
    he'd mix.

Initiation rites were not for him, Old Tom he'd disappoint.
The old ways were ignored, the 'Revolution' had occurred;
the pressures were all to conform to a new life with its new
    norms.
The young were free to choose new ways, the boundaries
    were blurred.

Billy with his slim stockman's build, seventeen and confident,
moleskin trousers and check shirt, broad hat and broad smile,
knew how to break in a horse and how to handle cattle
but older Nancy broke him in, with her experience and her
    guile!

A stockman on Nilpinna, Anna Creek and Hamilton –
well known on Kidman properties, his adult life had begun,
a young family at home with Nancy – Alison, Julie and Mark,
up at first light riding – life on a cattle run.

3. Abminga and Macumba, the Stockman's Life

To Abminga siding, on the Ghan, the Bailes brothers would retire.
They took their wives and built new lives, running a busy store.
Cooper was now with Daisy, sisters in an extended family;
soon baby June was born, a sister for brother Billy.

Cooper no longer went on cattle musters, many old friends had died –
no more spirits with old mate Ted Lennon.
Alcohol robbed him of his pride
and when June joined the 'Stolen Generations', past happiness was forgotten.

Life did not work out with Nancy, she moved away to Finke.
Billy worked for George Birchmore, another Kidman man.
George managed Macumba, a property where Ernie Kempe
had been a famous figure – tough, rough but still a human!

Rex Lowe of Mt Dare station was as hard as granite rock.
Billy recalls he was a 'cheeky bloke', tough on Black or White.
He'd tie them to a post or tree if they crossed his path
and there he'd belt them with a whip – not a pleasant sight.

Around campfires and homesteads, stories were told of Mr Lowe.
'Barbed wire Jack' came to Mt Dare, via the mines at Tennant Creek.
Looking for work, he boasted to Rex that he could ride so well –
it was his first mistake, as Rex organised a little treat.

Out came a horse. 'Let's see ya ride,' calmly said old Rex.
Young Jack soon found himself bucked off and lying in the dust.
Rex promptly showed him how to ride and Jack said, 'Can you fight?'
Rex touched him up with hardened knuckles, but let him stay to work.

All men on the station had their favourite horse.
Billy recalled some famous rides – there were some famous faces.
Who could forget 'flash' Johnny Cadell, resplendent in silk shirts
as he graced the dusty tracks at rodeos and bush races.

Janet Stewart worked on Macumba, a domestic or servant girl.
Billy soon 'went out with her' and asked for permission to marry.
Across in Oodnadatta, forms were duly filled
and in the old school house, police performed the wedding ceremony.

Months out in the bush, droving down the tracks,
card games when the sun went down, somewhere in the outback
miles from 'civilisation', life was very simple.
Don't let the bullocks stray too far, keep the herd intact!

The drover in dusty trousers, wide hat and 'cowboy' shirt –
hot sun in early morning, the sky a brilliant blue.
The ancient land goes on forever – no sign of modern man.
Billy's on his beige horse Trigger, packhorse Stockman follows too.

Thin mist in the winter hovers low along the valleys;
shimmering silver mirages lie like lakes on the desert plains.
The stars of the Milky Way shine brighter than city lights
and smoke from a lone campfire disappears into the night.

The muster nearly over, the cattlemen will soon be home;
fresh meat at the homestead – a change from bully beef.
Now the men can wash away the dust and sweat and grime
with a change of clothes, and women – at last some light relief!

Billy remembers the 'good life', with 'fresh air' and 'plenty of tucker',
the ever-changing scenery, sandhills and gibber plains,
the blue leaves of the saltbush, the yellow blades of Mitchell grass,
the red earth of the desert, the soft purples of the distant range.

4. Oodnadatta and Contact with Adelaide

Twenty years on Macumba, six children needing school –
Billy retired to Oodnadatta, where once the gidgee grew.
A short time later, terrible tragedy for all –
Janet dead in a car accident, the years together seemed so few.

Life went on in Oodnadatta, though some moved away
son Cooper, on a bike, chasing cattle 'cross plain and ridge.
'The young ones got it easy,' Billy would say to me.
'Life with electricity and machines and fresh food in the fridge.'

Many years later, a reunion for Billy and sister June.
For close on half a century, their lives had been apart,
June brought up in Adelaide, Billy in the bush,
living in two different worlds, now for a new start.

I lived in the Alice, I met old Bill and Cooper.
Cooper died in '63 and Bill two years later.
Cooper I knew only for a few weeks – his life was almost over.
Bill said he was 'a little wild', but never a mention of a child!

Strange how the name Cooper would bring us all together.
My grandfather was Cooper, brother to John the Squatter.
Billy's grandfather John had named his youngest Cooper
while my grandpa named my father John – what pattern
    could be simpler!

My cousin John had a son, Jason was his name.
From Queensland to Adelaide he returned and checked the
    electoral roll.
Imagine his surprise when he found a Cooper Bailes at Oodnadatta.
His newborn son was Cooper, Coincidence? Could that be all?

My father John rang me, to check the family tree.
Nothing seemed apparent, but the name sounded right.
A telephone call to Oodnadatta found young Cooper on the
    phone.
Soon all the pieces were in place – the Bailes were Black and
    White!

And so I'd talk to Billy, many a tale he would relate
and when he came to Adelaide, for his sister June was here,
I hastily arranged a meeting, a gathering of the clan.
It was quite fascinating to meet after all those years.

He spoke with a deep, rasping voice, the result of years of
    smoking.
'Aboriginal English' described his preferred linguistic style.
He always had a laugh and kept his sense of humour
although his life had been quite hard, with many a difficult
    trial.

Billy would recall days of his youth – the memories of yesteryear,
the last great corroborees of '48, and riding around Macumba,
Old Cooper and his 'log cabin tin', stockmen smoking by the
    fire,
Mother Mary talking to him in the languages of the Centre.

'Why do you walk with a limp?' asked our daughter Anna.
Billy told the story of how he was 'chasing brumbies around'.
His horse tripped on a rabbit hole; he was thrown off balance,
one leg caught in the stirrup, Billy dragging along the ground.

By the time he managed to stop his horse, the damage was already done.
A good day's ride from the homestead, his ankle badly broken,
Billy made it back eventually; it was a difficult journey.
By the time a doctor looked at him, his leg had set misshapen.

And what of Reconciliation, Billy? And National Sorry Day?
Billy gave a laugh and said, 'There's plenty to be sorry for.'
Legal words, policies from afar, solutions from above,
dollars misspent by bureaucrats, history's lessons all but ignored.

'David, it's simple,' Billy would say, his voice suddenly quite serious.
'The Whitefellas buggered up everything, the people and the land.
They never listen to what the Blackfellas want, they just don't understand.
They have their money and their jobs, while our kids play in the sand.'

Of all the introduced species, the White man was the worst.
He introduced the feral weeds and feral animals too.
He spread disease across the land, set up 'Protection Boards',
stole women for his pleasure and left poison in the food.

A people dispossessed of all, a people robbed of their culture.
Too late the governments reacted; some missions tried their best
to save the Aboriginal languages and give health care to the needy,
but government policies made life worse, as poverty and anger will attest.

Remember the famous desert landscapes of Albert Namatjira
praised all around the world, recognised by all the nation.
Albert was given the right to drink – an 'honorary citizen'
but when he shared his alcohol he was put in prison!

The poisonous clouds of Maralinga, the radioactive land,
messages dropped to Desert dwellers – pity they couldn't read.
The Cold War years and A-bomb tests, the politics of fear,
White Australia under pressure, Land Rights described as greed.

Vietnam, votes and protest songs, Mabo and Gurrindji.
There were some gains and recognition for the need for Reconciliation.
But Billy tired of all the talk, not backed up by any actions.
His people lived in poverty, where even the young were dying.

The old men no longer sing the rain – and we are left with Global Warming.
The boozing life brings nothing but strife – bored minds turn to drug taking.
Daughter Suzanne's 'got problems with her kids…Welfare call round'.
Bobby and Donna are 'doing all right' – Janice and Tanya 'OK in town'.

Donna and I chat on the phone, when Billy's not around.
There's hope for the future – 'Young Raghi's real good at sport.'
Michael Long the footballer went on his long awareness walk.
New initiatives for young people – 'Maybe Raghi'll play for
    Port.'

Sometimes Billy rings me and calls me 'cousin' or 'brother'.
We discuss the family and laugh about the past.
'I'm Black and White,' says Billy. 'I'm a fair dinkum
    Australian.'
Reconciliation real for us, Billy no longer a 'half-caste'

'A lot of bad things happened in the past,'
Billy would say to me.
'These days life is better' – but problems still remain.
'Things can improve,' said Billy, 'if White blokes used their
    brain!'

Too many brothers behind bars, sisters victims of abuse.
Too many children in YP lands sniffing petrol from a can.
Education of the nation and more commonsense conversation
must take priority in policy that will see positive interaction.

5. Eringa, 2005

Last time I talked to Billy, he'd been here and there.
He talked of a little 'homeland' out on a Williams station.
He'd given up claim to Federal, now Crown land again
He'd been back to Eringa, to the lands of the Perentie Nation.

The grey-green eucalypts hug Eringa waterhole.
Graceful pelicans glide into the water as in days of old.
A crowd of zebra finches cheep happily at the water's edge
where the gentle waves lap and suck against the blackened roots of the bank.

Skid marks in the desert, fish killed by dynamite.
Billy surveys the scene still hoping for a future
where life will return and the land will show recovery
from the long years of torment, without protection from its people.

Miniri the Thorny Mountain Devil basks upon a rock
blending into the desert with oranges, browns and red
lifting up a head, so weird and wonderful
where the hint of a smile promises a brighter world ahead.

Tjukurr, Ngura, Kurrunpa – Walytja and Kanyini.
Dreaming-Law, Land-Place-Home, the Spirit – Soul has meaning
for Family and the People in their care-connection.
All the bonds must be renewed for the future of the nation.

Elizabeth Bailes and children John, William, baby Cooper, Frank, Mary. Yorkshire, 1870.

Cooper Bailes and Emily Maud Bailes (Barrow). Yorkshire, c. 1878.

*John and and Mary Bailes.
Bloods Creek, c. 1895.*

Camel caravan, late 1800s.

John Bailes and wife Louise (Gowans). Federal Station, c.1910.

John Bailes and sons Bill and Cooper. Federal Station, c. 1920.

Rosie – Indurkuta, the desert rose – with Bailes goats. Bloods Creek.

Wedding of Old Bill Bailes. Wife Faye with Les Jones and Gertie Gumley.

Billy, Cooper and Bobby Bailes. Macumba, c. 1979.

Billy the stockman.

Len, Ethel and eight children.

David with Molly Lennon.

Gravestone of Cooper Bailes. Alice Springs.

Gravestone of Old Bill Bailes (Rudd). Alice Springs.

Bronco busting. Billy Bailes on horse. Allandale, 1976.

Ngintaka the perentie.

Dalhousie Springs.

The sacred spring of Ngintaka. Eringa Hills.

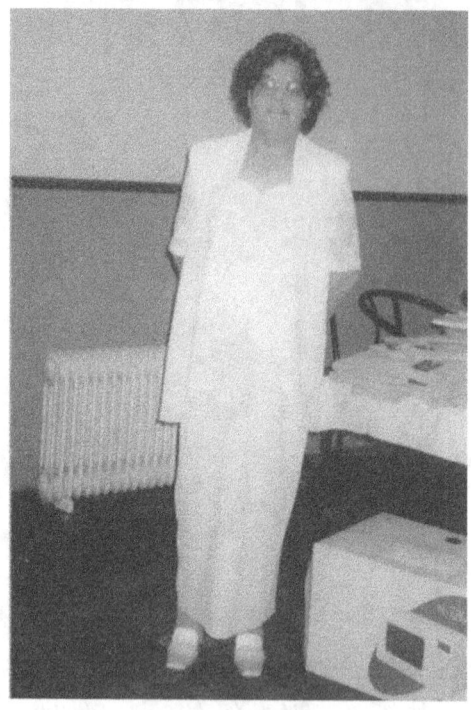

Reunion, 2002. Billy, David, June, Tanya Bailes.

June Bailes, wedding.

*June's daughter Vicki Long
and baby Kiara.*

Len finds his friends...but his family history is just a painful blank

'BURIED' BY THE BUNGALOW

PEOPLE went to the Back to Bungalow reunion at Alice Springs recently for many reasons. For Len Bell, now in his 60s, it was another chance to unlock the secrets of his past.

Like hundreds of other mixed-race children from central Australia and even as far as Darwin, Len was taken from his family and placed in one of three "Bungalow" compounds for "half-caste" children which operated in Alice Springs from the mid 1920s until 1942.

Len, who was taken from his home at Charlotte Waters, near the SA-Northern Territory border at the age of two, has 88 grandchildren and great-grandchildren, but still does not know who his mother and father were, or whether he has brothers and sisters.

He has been searching all his life for his parents.

Len, who now lives in Cloncurry, Qld, says the Bungalow reunion for him was another chance to find that vital lead.

His last contact with most of the people who could know his past was in 1956 when, as a nine year-old, he was taken from the Bungalow and sent to Croker Island off the northern Australian coast.

Len, Ethel and family. Bungalow, Alice Springs.

Len and Billy first reunion. Oodnadatta, 2007.

The Honourable Kevin Rudd MP
Prime Minister
requests the pleasure of the company of
Lennie Bell
at a Morning Tea on the occasion of the
National Apology to the Stolen Generations
to be held by leave of the Presiding Officers
in the Members' Hall, Parliament House
on Wednesday, 13 February 2008, at 10.15 am – 11.30 am

To Remind

Please present this card on arrival

Dress: Lounge Suit
Day Dress
Smart Casual

Len Bailes (Bell). Sorry Day invitation.

Jim Ferry (Marutju), wife Cecilia, David and Janice Bailes, 2006.

John Bailes (sister Cornelia in background) and children Julia, David, Cecilia and Matthew, 2001.

David and Billy Bailes, 2007.

Billy Bailes memory eulogy cover, 2013.

David and Cooper Bailes at Billy's funeral, 2013.

Red and White dingo pups – the Breakaways.

Simpson Desert dunes.

Uluru.

3

Assimilation and the Impact of the 'Stolen Generations'

Patrol 235 Charlotte Waters

May the fourth, 1934.
Constable Kennett of Charlotte Waters
checked his supplies and his orders
and readied the camels and the horses.

Trackers Mick Doolan and Johnny Hayes
were Arrernte men with a keen eye.
They read the tracks across the sand
for this was their country and their home.

A wire from the Alice had instructions –
'Give rations to the old and infirm Abos,
check reports of VD suspects in the area
and round up any half-caste children.'

Jack Kennett farewelled his pregnant wife.
They had four children under ten;
sometimes for weeks he'd be away
but this time he planned to return that night.

Forty miles a day out on patrol
across stony flats and desert dunes.
The old and infirm were easily found,
White man's rations replacing lost desert food.

Monday morning the seventh of May.
Police patrol 235 on New Crown station
were told their VD suspects were long gone
'somewhere in the bush in South Australia'.

On the same morning deep in the desert
a campfire burned in the Finke's broad bed.
A family in tattered dust-coloured clothes
ate damper beneath the river red gums.

Mary, a young mother, held her son.
They spoke the languages of the Centre.
Her boy Lenny, not yet two, had been born
to a white man known as 'Aba'.

The laws of the land were quite clear.
A White man with a Black woman was taboo
but Aba would sleep with anyone
regardless of age or race.

Aba had met Mary on Federal Station.
He understood ngapartji-ngapartji.
'I give to you and your family
and you can come and sleep with me.'

Aba had never been part of Lenny's life
and now Lenny's world would drastically change.
Three mounted men followed the footprints,
hunting 'half-castes' as if they were game.

Constable Kennett was following orders –
a man with a gun, the law on a camel.
Young Lenny forced from his mother's grasp,
her screams her last contact with her son.

While Constable Kennett rode into the distance,
Mary threw off her ragged clothes.
With a jagged rock she gashed her head
and bright red blood splashed on her naked chest.

Lenny's cries and tears were to no avail.
Held fast by a strong arm on the saddle,
no more would he hear his mother's voice
and there would be no memories of his family.

The next train to the Alice took Lenny away.
He'd become a 'Bungalow' boy.
But at age nine he was sent far north
to Croker Island – a Methodist mission.

Lenny would grow up far from the Centre.
'God's word' replaced the Dreaming stories
and well-meaning Methodist missionaries
cared for him, one of the 'Stolen Generations'.

Boy From the Centre in the North

Lenny aged ten lived on Croker Island –
the home of the Iwaidja north-east of Darwin.
Mission English was his means of communication
and none of his family were blood relations.

There were pleasant memories of island life
like the time Timothy made him a kapok canoe
and far from the settlement he'd paddle to places
where tropical fish could be easily speared.

Wild ponies gave the children free rides
when chores were finished and the garden done.
Billygoat plums and wild blackcurrants
were just some of the foods found in the bush.

In February '42, planes flew overhead,
the rising sun symbol on their sides.
The children waved, not knowing these pilots
were on course for Darwin with their bombs.

The lugger *Larrpan* – a Methodist boat –
took the children and their carers across the sea.
The Reverend Kentish was friendly and practical
and helped organise transport south.

The Kakadu region was hardly a park
with its dangerous swamps and crocodiles
but even though the children had to walk
they could swim and play in exotic lagoons.

For this was a place of natural beauty
with ranges and plains and thick vegetation
full of waterbirds, buffalo and native animals,
with ancient paintings on cliffs and caves.

There were lighter moments on the trek
as on one day the girls were quite surprised
when the elastic from their panties disappeared,
having been made into shanghais by the boys!

The children and adults eventually arrived
at Birdum, a small town on the Stuart Highway.
From there they could safely continue their journey
on military trucks and from the Alice on rail.

Eventually the convoy arrived at Otford,
a small town in the Blue Mountains.
There they lived until the war ended
and then returned by boat to Croker Island.

On the island Lenny worked on pineapple plantations.
One day he finally left the Mission;
he travelled south – drawn to the Centre
but in the Alice there were no clues.

Droving cattle for Lord Vestey,
Lenny wondered, 'Who am I?' and 'Where am I from?
Did my father care that I had gone?'
And 'Was my mother still alive?'

2008, Reunion and Reconciliation

Two brothers stood in a dusty street
late in May in Oodnadatta.
For seventy years they had been apart,
not knowing they shared the same Black mother.

'Hello, brother' were the first words
Lenny heard spoken by Billy
and after years of searching Lenny reached out
to physically bond with his blood family.

Lenny and Billy had been born in the thirties
around Bloods Creek and New Crown station,
Their mother Mary from the lands of the Luritja
had worked as a maid for two White brothers.

Mary had lost Lenny before he was two –
taken by police and sent far away,
for children born to Black and White parents
had been put on lists for institutions.

Youngest son Billy had remained safe on the station
protected by family – Black and White.
Billy's first languages were not English
and he had retained his cultural ties.

For years Lenny had looked for lost family
and many times visited Alice Springs.
One time, he had taken his children and wife Ethel
to a 'Bungalow' reunion to unlock the past.

A break would come with information
from old archives and a police report.
Lenny had been taken near Charlotte Waters
with tracker Mick Doolan in a leading role.

Once more Lenny returned to the Alice
with his sons – Ronnie and Paul.
Lloyd Kyle from KASH and others from LINK-UP
were part of a group full of hope.

In Finke, Lenny met Richard Doolan
the grandson of Mick, the famous tracker.
The Doolan clan explained to Lenny
a police mistake – 'not Bell's son but Bailes'!'

The years of wondering were now over;
Lenny at last had found his family.
In Oodnadatta he was reunited with Billy
and visited the grave of their mother Mary.

Two things had always troubled Lenny;
one was not knowing about his kin,
the other the failure of leaders in government
to help heal the wounds of the 'Stolen Generations'.

Now Lenny enjoyed the February apology
as an invited guest of Prime Minister Rudd
but while not yet ready to forgive the past
his spirit calmed with a sense of peace.

Lenny had found Billy and extended family;
he had returned to the ancestral lands.
He knew now where he was from
in a year of reunion and reconciliation.

June and the 'Stolen Generations'

For I was hungered, and ye gave me no meat: I was thirsty, and ye gave me no drink:
I was a stranger, and ye took me not in: naked, and ye clothed me not: sick, and in prison, and ye visited me not.
– Matthew 25:42

1. Central Australia, mid-1900s

'I turned out all right,' says June with a laugh and a smile.
'No point being negative, or getting all depressed.'
Life goes on and Colebrook Home remains a distant memory
where once the Sisters made clothes and checked all were
well dressed.

June's White father Cooper, the former cattleman,
lived with two Aboriginal sisters – they were in his care.
They lived and worked together, running an outback store
but Cooper's alcoholism would leave his family in despair.

Cooper had protected son Billy from the clutches of Welfare.
Billy had learned to ride and was useful on a station.
Welfare had decided Billy was 'too old' and not in need of
    'special care'
but June was 'young' and 'vulnerable', parental drinking an
    excuse for 'action'.

And so Cousin June was part of the 'Stolen Generations',
taken from her Black mother at an early age.
White father Cooper had lived with her mother Daisy
in an 'illegal' relationship, in the far north of SA.

Abminga, the place of the 'snake track', was then a siding for
   the Ghan.
The metal tracks of the White man stretched across red sands.
Coming up from Oodnadatta – the place of the gidgee tree –
the Ghan carried cargoes, supplies and people, and took
children no longer free.

Three long days, and three long nights,
slowly, the Ghan wound its way south.
Farewell to the purple ranges, shimmering in the heat haze;
farewell to the blue-grey saltbush, scattered across orange earth.

Gone from the ancestral lands of the Arrernte, Luritja.
Where were her grandparents, Malu and Pundi?
Who would tell her the stories of the Perentie Dreaming?
Would she know she was a tjitji, now robbed of her kanyini?

No longer would she smell the sweet rain of the summer
nor a father's whisky breath – nor the smell of a mother.
Gone the smell of a campfire – gone the smells of poverty;
farewell to the mysteries of the vast outback, farewell the
   smell of liberty!

2. Colebrook Home, Adelaide, 1950s

Leaving Colebrook Home in 1952,
Sister Hyde and Sister Rutter had shown genuine Christian concern.
Replaced by other families and so-called 'Christian' workers,
life at Colebrook Home often took a far more sinister turn.

'Lord, make us truly thankful for what we are about to receive.'
Such were the words of a grace, repeated every day by all.
The Fincks and their daughters, well-meaning missionaries,
would replace distant grieving mothers whose lives were in turmoil.

June missed older brother Billy – no more 'mothers' in the home.
Barefoot in the desert, now in shiny shoes,
all dressed up for Sunday – Christianity with little joy,
children firmly disciplined; some, victims of abuse.

There were some lighter moments – children united by a common fate.
Games were played like hopscotch, hide-and-seek and kick the tin.
The children recalled their Desert words, although their languages were lost.
Sometimes there were visits to church youth groups and lollies when guests came in.

Taken away to 'a better life,' was the conventional wisdom;
'half-caste' boys and 'half-caste' girls needed rapid
    assimilation.
Aboriginal Protector Neville hoped to 'breed out all the
    colour'.
To make 'Black' children 'White' would give them a place
    within the nation.

What place in Australia for the first Australian people?
The 'White Australia' policy was alive and practised very well.
Non-Whites were not welcome in a land where Non-Whites
    lived –
racism enshrined in laws that reflected the White man's will.

A small, frightened girl alone in Colebrook Home –
with whom can she share her hopes and her fears?
Can a carer replace a lost mother's love?
Can friends replace a brother or understand the tears?

So many children traumatised in so many different ways –
removed from their familiar land with its sacred sites and stories,
forbidden to speak their languages or mix with 'full-blood'
    family,
a devastating loss of culture and major problems with identity.

So who were these lost little children, living in a home?
'Half-caste' was a common term – a demeaning, misleading term;
children whose skin was too dark to be 'White',
their Aboriginal heritage denied, robbed of their birthright.

European settlement meant that wealthy Whites took away the land.
Economic rationalism put Aboriginal people last.
Families were suffering with disease, hunger and abuse,
yet the children were taken away when support was needed most.

Many of the 'Stolen Generations' would carry burdens from the past –
guilt, anger and low esteem would create problems in future years.
Violence, depression and alcohol abuse would take a terrible toll.
Help and Reconciliation came too late for those who were left to grieve.

Schools taught students about the kings and queens of England,
adjectival clauses and the finer points of punctuation.
Anzacs fighting for the 'Motherland' – the First Fleet at Botany Bay.
Aboriginal students were not 'academic', only good with 'physical education'.

Such was the curriculum in the state and private schools,
and the 'hidden curriculum' manifested blatant forms of racism.
Italians and Greeks were the butt of many schoolyard jokes
but Australia's first inhabitants endured even greater taunts.

June's school years would quickly pass – soon she'd be at work.
There she'd meet Patricia, who took her home for tea.
Patricia's parents, George and Pat, invited her to stay;
at last she had acceptance, in a caring family.

3. Adelaide, 1960s and Beyond: Reunion

Growing in confidence, June worked at Clarks and Anglicare,
living with the down-to-earth Grahams in Hyde Park.
June made inquiries about brother Billy, up in Oodnadatta,
the Bailes surname easily traced, well known in those
    northern parts.

Billy was on Macumba station, a stockman in the saddle.
He'd recently married Janet, their family life had just begun.
He came down from 'up north', a bushman in the city,
and met up with his sister June, far from his cattle run.

So many years had passed; Billy's life had been so different.
He was closer to his roots, his family and the land.
Even when he talked, he spoke a different language.
He had not been taken on a one-way ticket on the Ghan.

Reunion for the children of the 'Stolen Generations'
stirs all the hidden emotions and all the deep hurts.
So many could not find their long-lost loved ones;
others, plagued by guilt and doubt, wondered if reunion
    could really work.

In the early seventies June gave birth to daughter Vicki.
A single mother, she was persuaded to give her baby girl away.
In a not-so-strange way, history repeated itself –
a mother and daughter apart, sadness on many a day.

Many years later June and Vicki would meet again,
Vicki a young woman with a baby of her own.
Little Kiara Amy would meet a welcoming grandmother
but after friendly contacts, Vicki stopped coming to June's home.

In later life June married, to Noel of Scots descent.
For some time she had lived at Goodwood, next to a busy tramline.
Nursing duties with Anglicare, June worked hard for many a year,
contacts with her adopted parents and with Billy from time to time.

A Cooper living in Adelaide, a Cooper living in Oodnadatta.
Family history inquiries would lead me to Billy and June.
Social and economic factors had kept our family apart.
Relationships severed in the past could now be given a new start.

The prime minister talks of multiculturalism, of rights for all our citizens –
millions of dollars spent on Iraq and super for politicians,
'compo' paid to victims of crime and those in accidents,
but what of the plight and condition of our Indigenous population?

June and I keep in touch and tell of family news.
When I umpire near her place, she comes to watch the game.
'Hey ump, there's an old Aboriginal lady, calling your name,'
says a young White footballer, when I'm in the room to change.

Interesting how the colour of your skin influences perceptions.
It does dictate how we relate and how we think of others.
Too many people have irrational fears, based on misconceptions
but you and I are just the same – sisters and brothers in one
 nation.

We have NAIDOC Week, Sorry Day and talk of Reconciliation.
All that is fine and education will help reduce aspects of racism.
Awareness of problems that still exist for most Aboriginal people
can only be solved with persistence and two-way communication.

The long list of disastrous policies of the past must be understood
so that in the present and the future, mistakes will not be
 repeated.
For a prime minister not to say 'sorry' tells us of his thinking.
We remember killing fields overseas, but at home nothing is
 admitted.

Many people sympathise with the girls in *Rabbit-proof Fence*.
'It was a great movie,' comments one. 'How sad they were
 taken away.'
The 'Stolen Generation' are still here; so many families suffered,
their story another sad chapter in a long and tragic play.

Truth and Reconciliation can have great impact on a nation.
South Africa suffers as Black and White shed tears upon the
 stage.
Here in Australia, Reconciliation lacks political direction
as practical considerations are ignored, and problems still rage.

There has been regeneration for the 'Stolen Generations'
with recognition of their culture, at home and overseas.
Part of being Australian is in their contribution
of their arts and culture, which has set their spirit free.

Colebrook Home is gone – in its place a fountain
unveiled by Lowitja – The Fountain of Tears.
Doris has her 'rock', with its touching inscription
'We are the stolen children who were taken away.'

The journey of healing is helping the sisters.
Sadly, many of the brothers no longer remain.
The *Grieving Mother* unveiled by past Colebrook children
tells the story of Muriel's mother and of a family's pain.

Many of the Colebrook girls have overcome their problems;
they have taken a successful place in our community.
June and I have had our long-overdue reunion.
'Yes, June, you did turn out all right,' I say most happily.

I throw my arm around my cousin – Black and White together.
'I'll catch up with you soon,' I say as I'm about to leave.
I know that June has suffered much – much is left unsaid.
The wounds run deep, but she is strong, and hope still lies ahead.

Colebrook Reserve is now a place of Reconciliation.
Black and White magpies there have no problems with their colour.
'Know ye the truth, and the truth will set you free.'
David and June – you and I – our place in History.

Vale Cousin June

Cousin June always had a smile
and when at times we'd say goodbye
she'd speak to me in her familiar way.
'See you later, cousin – love you, David.'

Five years were all we had together,
reunited after half a century,
for she was part of the 'Stolen Generations'
taken from her mother, north of Oodnadatta.

We were so close, like brother and sister;
we made up for all the years apart.
Our relationship for us was so special.
I was blood family from her past.

We often chatted on the phone.
We'd laugh about her brother Billy.
She'd tell me how life was with Noel
and I'd keep her posted on our family.

The pale pink lilies are in full flower.
June cannot see them any more
and as she passes from this world,
friends and family hold her hand.

Her last few days saw monsoonal rain
come from the north where rivers raged,
bringing life back to where once she came
and there the awakening desert daisies celebrate her name.

Ningtaka the powerful Perentie Man
will welcome home one of his own
and like fead finish after rain
her soul will bloom deep in the desert terrain.

4

Reunion and Reflection

The Finke Mob

Driving down to Oodnadatta
crammed in cars 'cross corrugations
come the Finke mob.

Noisier than parrots at a waterhole,
writhing in a mass like sawfly larvae,
the Finke mob stick to the railway station.

The hot red sun sets over the Neales,
the heat of the day fast fades away
while desert voices party in the warm night air.

Here the words of Arrernte and Yankunytjatjara
mix with well-known English words and phrases.
'You're just an old fuckin' whore,' shouts a drunken man.

Two women pass on the sandy street.
'Is Julie at the station?' I enquire.
'I'm Billy Bailes's cousin and she's his daughter.'

A young Black woman staggers towards me.
'I'm related to Billy on the Stewart side,'
and she points to the crowd where Julie can be found.

Djewi Geoff has misgivings as we near the noise.
'Don't worry, mate,' I quickly say.
'They're part of my family and they're here today!'

I approach a lady with a VB can.
'Is Julie here, Billy Bailes' daughter?'
'Julie,' she yells, and Julie appears.

'I'm Billy's cousin,' I begin to say.
Julie gives me a rough, drunken embrace.
'Uncle David,' she says, 'come and meet some more.'

I say, 'Let's get a photo together.'
Julie talks to others in the crowd.
'Cousin David,' says one. 'Brother David,' calls another.

A young boy in shorts with tousled hair
is hoisted high by a stocky Black man.
'Take our picture together,' Julie pleads.

The woman with the can completes the frame.
I take a shot and hear Geoff say,
'Hey, isn't that Billy – just over there?'

'Tjilpi kuta,' I call out to Billy.
My 'elder brother' is quite calm
in his blue and white checked shirt and stockman's hat.

Geoff takes a picture of family and friends.
I talk to tall Robert in an orange shirt.
He has long wavy hair and a soft thoughtful voice.

Once more we take a picture of 'the boys'.
'Where's marutju?' says Billy with a little smile.
'My brother-in-law's busy at our camp,' I say.

Voices call out, 'Hey, brother, come here.'
'Can you take our picture?' 'Do you have a beer?'
But as Billy said, 'They're too drunk for me!'

Geoff and I say that we must go.
'Goodbye, Julie.' 'We'll talk again some time.'
Julie clings to me like a long-lost friend.

As we walk away, the voices rise and fall.
The party will continue long into the night.
While the pensions are paid, the beer will flow.

I'd love to stay and talk to all.
What are their hopes? And what of their fears?
Is their culture lost? Is their future bleak?

A once-proud people lay drunk in the dust.
Government policies 'Bloody rubbish,' says Billy the Stockman.
'The people have nothing and no bastard cares.'

Kinship still matters; for each other they care.
The land is important with its sacred sites.
Perhaps a new generation will find a new way and rekindle
   hope before it's too late.

The night is now cool and a campfire burns.
The smoke rises towards the glittering stars
where the soul expands into the vastness of space.

Julie and Billy, Donna and Cooper,
they are my brothers, they are my sisters.
Finke, Oodna and Adelaide – different worlds yet still the same.

The mongrel dogs sleep with the Finke mob
in the middle of the desert on the red-orange sand,
and everything is held in the healing silence of this magical,
    mysterious outback land.

Black Man/White Man – Red Blood

Dreamtime – White time
red land – green land
Black man – White man
paths will cross.

Aluritja Desert country, Yorkshireman-rolling Dales
windbreak shelter – three-storey farmhouse
bark canoe – footprints in the sand, sailing ship – camel train
two different lands.

Cleanskin Tom – Old Man John
hunter, gatherer – borer, squatter
campfires, creek beds – bottle floors, tin roof
life from the land.

Emus, perenties – cattle, horses
bush tracks, bush tucker – fences, property
our land, with the land – my land, on the land
land under pressure.

Natural springs – nardoo seed – water tanks, flour bags
kangaroo, honey ants – bully beef – whisky, beer
long coats, barefoot – broad-brim hat, stockman's boots
blurred boundaries – blurred vision.

Respect the elders – respect the boss
learn the old stories – hear the padre preach
rules for living – White man's law
culture clash and culture crushed.

Black eyes, black bodies – blue eyes, red necks
bare breasts – cover up
Black woman – White man
new coloured generations.

Drought, flood, fire, famine
rich man, poor man, beggarman, thief
lust in the dust – bones in the desert
police in vans and tears on the sand.

Cooper Creek – Cooper's brew
Mary's child – Cooper's son
Billy the stockman – Kidman's run
Black you lose – White you win.

Children laughing – mothers crying
children playing – children lost
children hiding – charcoal faces
Daisy, Cooper, drown their sorrow.

Fresh air, cattle whips – city smog, car horns
spinifex, red gum – four walls, tall buildings
purple distances, red sunsets – grey roads, bright lights
Billy under the stars and June in Colebrook Home.

Ancient land – ancient history
spear, bullet – friend and foe
new land and new beginnings
new children live and new lives grow.

The lean old warriors have long since gone.
Gallipoli and Buna claim their heroes and dead,
give them food and give them tobacco.
Black and White grow fat together.

Bars to racism – racism in bars
hands that help – words that hurt
footy stars and Desert dot painting
family reunion – David meets June.

Understand the tears – allay the fears
not sorry on one day – begin today
we can't change the past but change we must
for Reconciliation Days are the future ways.

Conversations with My Late Brother Billy

A text message on a mobile phone
informed me Billy had passed away,
and while the news was no surprise
I'd always hoped for one last meeting.

Our families were people of the Centre
with Bailes a well-known pioneering name.
However, old tjamu Tom and kami Pundi
had connections way back to the Tjukur Dreaming.

Billy was my beloved kuta,
a much-respected elder brother
but on the phone I'd have to yell
for pina pati Billy was hard of hearing.

When calling Billy in Oodnadatta
I'd say, 'Wai nyuntu palya kuta'
and even when ill he'd reply
'Palya' in a deep, strong tone.

I would ask him what he did in hospital
and with a laugh or cough he'd simply say,
'Nothing – there's nothing to do in here
except eat good tucker and watch the kungka.'

Sometimes Billy called with special requests.
'David,' he'd say, 'I want a car.'
'A Toyota is what I really need.
See if you can find one – and send it up.'

Other times he'd talk of his garden
and ask for wire for his geese.
'I want them fat for Christmas time,
just like my old man Cooper did on the station.'

We'd talk about people from the past
and I would mention names to Billy.
He'd say old so-and-so was 'all right'
while some were 'cheeky' and others 'good blokes'.

I'd ask Billy if there had been rain.
'Kapi wiya' was his usual answer
but in times when there'd been heavy falls
Billy recalled the grasses, bush tucker and waterholes.

Billy was very proud of his family,
often talking of his sons and daughters,
and he'd joke about grandson Malachi saying,
'He'll find a kungka before his uncle Cooper!'

Soon I'll return to faraway Oodnadatta
to grieve with my brothers and my sisters
and our tears will fall on the soft red earth
as we farewell our father, brother and grandfather.

A hot wind will blow the eternal dust of the manta
and the ancient stone hills will guard the secret ceremonies,
for Billy will return to the lands of Ngintaka
where many have gone before and to where he belongs.

The Stockman's Funeral at Oodnadatta

The Anangu have come from the lands of the Centre
to bury Billy – a loved senior relative.

We are all shades of Black and White
but here today we are all one family.

A tearful grandson comes from Uluru
while Uncle Phillip leads the Finke mob convoy.

There are cousins from Indulkana on the Lands
and two handsome youths from New South Wales.

Billy's young granddaughters care for their children
while other barefooted tjitji have many mothers.

The crowd at the Oodnadatta Memorial Hall service
spill out onto the red sandy street.

I read the eulogy and a poem for Billy
and an elder from Finke speaks in wangka – language.

We bury Billy with his Kidman's hat
and his short stockwhip and old riding boots.

The man is gone but the memories remain
and all have their favourite and amusing stories.

The Bailes girls and in-laws work hard with the food,
preparing a feast that would've pleased their late father Billy.

I talk to Deano about Billy's Ngintaka Dreaming
and of how Ngintaka chased the sand goanna Milpali.

'You know, Dave, that's why Billy didn't eat Ngintaka
but he didn't mind a bit of roast Milpali!'

Deano tells me of how he went to Eringa with Billy
and of how Billy showed him the sacred rock sites.

We then talk of the Great Frog Dreaming
associated with the Luritja and Oodnadatta.

I say, 'Isn't it called the Nyanyi Dreaming?'
but Deano suddenly bursts into laughter.

'Dave,' he says, 'say Nganngi, not nyanyi,
or you're calling it the Women's Privates Dreaming!'

On a serious note, an annoyed Deano explains
that the school built a hall over a Frog Dreaming site.

Later Deano and I look at a photo of Billy on a horse
and recall Billy's love of his land and his people.

'He had a good life, Dave,' Deano tells me.
'He always worked hard and never complained.'

I know I'll miss my elder brother Billy
who advised me, 'Forget the city – just look at our stars.'

Reflections of a Bush Poet

this is where I am and will forever be
this is where I am from and where I will be going

the miracle of cellular division began the journey towards
  consciousness
of all that ever was and of all that will be known

I have seen the bright light coming from the beginning of time
and I have heard the familiar voices of those in a nearby realm

no need to rush towards a common fate
and no need to question that which is understood

scatter my ashes far from the constrictions of the city
and let my soul repose in the desert's eternal space

there my dust will mingle with the red sands of the Witjira
where the ever changing dunes always remain the same

here are the tracks and songlines of the powerful Ancestor Beings
telling the ancient stories of the world's first creation

on a warm summer's night the cries that are known to all
carry on the breeze fusing past and future

the broken down stardust of past brothers and sisters
has returned to the earth to create a new beginning

this is where I am and will forever be
this is where I am from and where I will be going

Appendix

Letters written by Cooper Bailes (Senior) to his brother Frank in England

Cooper was twenty years old and had recently arrived from the United Kingdom to work in the colony of South Australia. In 1890, Cooper worked with his elder brother John on the Nullarbor Plains in the far west of South Australia.

No. 4 Bore
Nullarbor Plains
Nov. 2nd/90

Dear Frank

I thought I would drop you a line to let you know how I am doing. It 1s a very long time since you wrote to me or Wm [William] either but it is quite excusable as I see by Maud's letter you have had more important business at hand. Well, I hope you like married life & have good luck with it. It will be Wm's [William's] turn next with the Ashby-de-la-Zouch young lady.

I have given up the sandalwood business & and am now with John at the No. 4 bore & am doing well. As soon as this bore is put down, I might go on a station for a while but a man never knows what he will do. You have to turn your hand to any mortal thing. Wm is travelling for a firm now and I think he will do very well. It is a healthy job for him travelling about the country. Maud will give you all particulars concerning the case.

I expect you will think you are never going to receive it but I shipped it by the first schooner bound for Albany and then by first steamer. I shall very likely return early in the next year but I hardly know yet. It all depends on what turns up. If I am doing well I might stay longer.

How are your stock looking & how does Sheldon like his farm at Queniborough & let me know how all the friends round there are & how farming is & everything. Let me know if the Miss Gilfords are married, also Miss Kidger, because if they are not, it would be advisable for them to come out here & they would very soon be on the list as Australia is very short of the female sex. I must now finish with love to your wife & yourself.

    I remain

        Your afcct. Brother

            Cooper.

The sandalwood that was selling for 7 & 8 [pounds] per ton is now almost valueless & I have 10 ton on my hands that I have cut, so it is a bit of a loss.

I have not heard from Wm for a long time so do not know how he is getting on. If I came home this year, I should most likely enlist in a good cavalry regiment. I should not care to live at home now after being away from it. John left his wife in Adelaide this time and I am very comfortable. John and I live in the house together. John has plenty of whiskey up here so altogether we do very well.

Well, I think I have told you all I know. I made a great mistake bringing a lot of new clothes out here with me. I was trying the jackets on today & they do not come halfway round me. So when I go to Adelaide, I shall have to walk about in my bush clothes till I can get a suit made.

I have never worn a coat or vest since I have been in the bush, only shirt trousers belt & boots.

I think I must conclude with love to yourself & wife and all.

I remain

    Your afcct. Brother

        Cooper.

Glossary

(Y) = Yankunytjatjara; (P) = Pitjantjatjara; (A) = Arrernte (Aranda)

Abminga (A): from apma-inga – place of the snake track; formerly a small railway siding, fettlers' camp and general store on the old Ghan railway

Alkarle (A): place of clear water; important Dreaming site (Perentie Dreaming)

Altyerrenge (A): Ancestor Beings from the Dreaming

Anangu (YP): person, people of the Western Desert, especially those in the Yankunytjatjara/Pitjantjatjara lands

Antakirinja: Western Desert language common around Coober Pedy and Oodnadatta

apara: eucalyptus camaldulensis; the famous river red gum found along river beds in Central Australia

Arabana: Aboriginal people associated with country west of Lake Eyre (Kati Thanda)

Arrernte (Aranda): Aboriginal people of Central Australia

Barcoo rot: a type of scurvy caused by a lack of fresh vegetables and fruit

bluebush: small desert bush with narrow leaves; blue-grey colour

cleanskin: not of 'mixed blood', that is, 'full blood', where both parents are Aboriginal; could also be used as a racist term

coolabah: eucalyptus microtheca; dense spreading gum tree common along the usually dry creek and river courses

dead finish bush: acacia tetragonophylla; kurara (Y); spiky acacia bush that appears dead in dry times but comes back to life after rain; seeds important food source for Central Desert peoples; new foliage may be eaten by cattle; also has medicinal qualities

desert dot painting: art style associated with paintings from the Western Desert area

djewi: origin unclear; term used by Western Desert Aboriginal people to describe a friend

Dieri: Aboriginal people from the eastern side of Lake Eyre

gidgee: Ikatuka (Y); large desert hardwood shrub or tree; an acacia common on flood plains and along dry creek beds; yellow wattle-like flowers, strong smell when wet; wood excellent for campfires; blue-grey drooping foliage

kalaya (Y): emu; important totemic animal

kandju (A): blue-tongue lizard

kanyini (YP): connection, look after, responsibility for

Kata Tjuta (YP): formerly known as the Olgas; dome-shaped mountains (literally, 'many heads') sacred to Aboriginal people of Central Australia

Kaurna: Aboriginal people of the Adelaide Plains/Adelaide area

kungka (Y): woman, female; sometimes slang for partner or girlfriend

kurun (Y): spirit, soul; n.b. kurunpa (P)

kurku (Y): mulga (hardwood tree, acacia); a general term

kuta (Y): brother, older brother

kwatye (A): water

Lhere Mparntwe (A): place of the river; River Todd, Alice Springs

lungkata (Y): blue-tongue lizard

Luritja/Aluritja: Western Desert language group; Aboriginal people of Central Australia

maku (Y): white grubs, witchetty grubs; found in acacia roots; prized traditional food

malu (Y): red kangaroo; important Ancestor Being and totemic symbol for men

mamu (Y): evil spirits. said to be active or dangerous at night or near waterholes

mangata (Y): quandong; santalum acuminatum; parasitic plant or tree with small bright red edible fruits; sometimes known as the desert peach; fragrant wood known as sandalwood

manta (Y): land, expanse of land

marutju (Y): brother-in-law; important person in kinship system

Milpali (Y): (say 'milbolyi') sand goanna; also a Dreaming Ancestor

miniri (Y): mountain devil/thorny devil lizard

Mparntwe (A): Alice Springs; contains many important Dreaming sites

mulga: acacia tree; extremely hard wood; often used for fencing

munyeroo (Dieri/Wongkanguru): edible succulent plant; seeds prized for making damper, a traditional bread cooked in a campfire

nardoo: origins unclear; ephemeral fern with seeds used for damper; John King, the sole survivor of the ill-fated Burke and Wills expedition, ate damper made from nardoo seeds

ngangkari (Y): traditional healers/doctors; highly skilled in use of traditional herbal remedies

ngankur wiya/nunkuria (Y): without a beard

Ngintaka (Y): the perentie/the Perentie Lizard Man; Australia's largest monitor lizard, growing up to three metres in length; associated with sacred sites around Bloods Creek; an important totemic symbol and Ancestor Creator being

ngura (Y): home, place, land locality

nyii-nyii (Y): the zebra finch; flocks seek protection from the spiky dead finish bush nyurka-nyurka (Y): thin, skinny; variation nyurkabina – skinny girl

parakeelya: Arabana/Yankunytjatjara (portulacca family); purple pink flowering succulent plant; leaves may be baked and eaten; common after rain

perentie: the giant goanna lizard; see also Ngintaka

Piranpa (P): White people; also Walypala (YP) – Whitefella

Pitjantjatjara: Aboriginal people of the Western Desert group in Central Australia; also known as the Anangu – the people

punti (Y): s(ay 'pundi'); desert cassia (senna) bush with yellow flowers; maku (grubs) also found in the roots of the punti bush

quandong: parasitic plant with edible fruit; see also mangata

river red gum: Eucalyptus camaldulensis; see also apara

ruby saltbush: euchyleana tomentosa; small bush with grey/blue leaves; small, edible ruby red fruits; plant may be eaten by livestock

saltbush: many varieties; small bush/shrub found in desert areas; salt-tolerant; very hardy; can be eaten by cattle, sheep and goats

tjala (Y): the honey ant; important traditional food source.; extended abdomen contains honey; an important totemic symbol often featured in Western Desert artworks

tjilpi (Y): elder/old man; a term of respect

tjitji (Y): children; a widely used term in the Western Desert regions; in South Australia often used by Aboriginal people to describe the children of the 'Stolen Generations'

Tjukur/Tjurkurpa (P): Dreaming/Dreamtime Law; a dynamic concept connecting past, present and future; an explanation of how life came to be; a word common to many Western Desert language groups

Uluru (YP): fomerly known as Ayers Rock, a giant monolith

with many sacred sites; very important to the
Yankunytjatjara and Pitjantjatjara people

Utna-datta (Arabana): known as Oodnadatta, place of the smelly or stinking gidgee/wattle; Oodnadatta was an important railway town on the old Ghan railway in the far north of South Australia

walytja/walytja-piti (Y): family, kin and family connections

wangka (YP): language, especially Western Desert language

Wapar (Y): Dreaming/Dreamtime/Dreaming Law; see also Tjukur

Warlpiri: Abroginal language group from Central Australia

wee-ai: young boy, youth; term taken from English by the Arrernte and used by other Central Australian groups

wiltja (P): shelter usually made from branches; commonly used by English speakers to describe an Aboriginal shelter even outside of Pitjantjatjara areas

Wirangu: Aboriginal people (Western Desert group) associated with the Nullarbor Plain

wintalyka (Y): acacia aneura, a type of mulga tree; seeds an important food source; hardwood used for tools and weapons

Wongkanguru: Aboriginal people of the far north-west of South Australia

Yankunytjatjara: Aboriginal people (Western Desert group) of Central Australia

Yeperenye (A): Giant Caterpillar People; Dreaming Ancestor Beings

Guidelines for pronunciation

Always stress the first syllable of each word.

'a' soft 'ar' as in cut

'k' often like a soft 'g' sound; for example, Kapi (water), say 'gapi' 'ng' as in sing; for example, Ngintaka (the perentie)

'p' often like a 'b' sound; for example, milpali (sand goanna), say 'milbolyi'

'r' rolled except when underlined or at the beginning of a word

'r' as in English word rock, not rolled; some syllables are almost swallowed; for example, Yankunytjatjara is pronounced 'Yunkunjara' and Pitjantjatjara is pronounced 'Pitinjara'.

't' often like a 'd' sound; for example, manta (land), say 'munda'

underlined _: curl tongue back in mouth as in tjuta (many)

Bibliography and Further Reading

The Adelaide Chronicle, 14 November 1925, obituary of Mr John Bailes

Bardon, Geoffrey, *Papunya Tula Art of the Western Desert*, JB Books Australia, 1999

Batty, Philip (ed.), *Colliding Worlds: First contact in the Western Desert 1932–1984*, Museum Victoria and National Aboriginal Cultural Institute, Tandanya, 2006

Brown, Ron, and Pat Studdy-Clift, *Bush Justice*, Hesperian Press, 1990

Douglas, W.H., *An introductory Dictionary of the Western Desert Language*, Institute of Applied Language Studies, W.A.C.A.E. Perth, 1988

Dunjiba Community Council Inc. and Jen Gibson, *Oodnadatta Genealogies*, Department of Environment and Planning, 1988.

Flood, Josephine, *The Original Australians: Story of the Aboriginal People*, Allen & Unwin, 2006

Grant, Arch, *Camel Train and Aeroplane (The story of Skipper Partridge)*, Rigby, 1981

Goddard, Cliff, *Pitjantjatjara/Yankunytjatjara to English Dictionary*, 2nd edition, Institute for Aboriginal Development, Alice Springs, 1992

Idriess, Ion L., *Cattle King*, Angus and Robertson, 1936

Johannsen, Kurt, *A son of 'The Red Centre'*, edited by Daphne Palmer. JB Books, South Australia, 1992

Kartinyeri, Doris, *Kick the Tin*, Spinifex Press, 2000

Kimber, R.G., *Man from Arltunga: Walter Smith, Australian Bushman*, Hesperian Press, 1986.

Mellor, Doreen, and Haebich, Anna, *Many Voices: Reflections on experiences of Indigenous child separation*, National Library of Australia, 2002.

Mountford, Charles P., *Brown Men and Red Sand*, Angus and Robertson, 1948

Muecke, Stephen, and Shoemaker, Adam, *Aboriginal Australians: First Nations of An Ancient Continent*, Thames and Hudson, 2004

Randall, Bob, *Songman: the story of an Aboriginal elder*, ABC Books, 2003

Shaw, Bruce, *Our Heart Is the Land: Aboriginal Reminiscences From the Western Lake Eyre Basin*, Aboriginal Studies Press, Canberra, 1995

Tur, Mona, *Cicada Dreaming*, Hyde Park Press, 2010